PROVIDING
Hope

LATIN AMERICA CHILDCARE

Life
Stories

Latin America **ChildCare**

ASSEMBLIES OF GOD WORLD MISSIONS

1445 Boonville Avenue • Springfield, MO 65802
Email: office@lacc4hope.org

www.lacc4hope.org
1.800.289.7071

ISBN 1-931940-90-8

© Copyright 2003 Latin America ChildCare

ALL RIGHTS RESERVED. No part of this book may be reproduced in any form without written permission of the publishers, except brief quotations used in connection with reviews in magazines or newspapers.

Dedication

*To the children whose lives have been
transformed through a relationship
with Jesus Christ and the caring sponsors
who have shared God's love with them!*

With deep gratitude

To John and Lois Bueno

Whose vision to reach the children in El Salvador
gave birth to a ministry that today touches
the lives of thousands of children in
Latin America and the Caribbean.

Whose faithfulness has inspired
missionaries and national leaders
to respond to the children in need.

To Doug and Myrna Petersen

Whose passion for the needy children has
been a lifetime commitment.

Whose dream fueled the expansion of the
ministry of Latin America ChildCare
to all parts of Latin America and the Caribbean.

Whose commitment gave birth to the
ministry of sponsorship enabling thousands
of caring people to give hope to needy children.

Whose love for the children is revealed
in the following stories, many of which Doug wrote.

Table of Contents

Foreword — i

Introduction — v

Chapter One: Changed by Salvation — 1

Chapter Two: Changed by Healing — 19

Chapter Three: Changed by Friends — 33

Chapter Four: Changed by Christ — 45

Conclusion — 87

Foreword

Why Latin America ChildCare? Can believers in the USA actually make a difference in the lives of needy children in Latin America? Aren't there too many lost children, and too much poverty for us to make a real impact?

You will find the answers to all these questions in the stories contained in the pages of this book, stories of powerful impact made by people just like you and me, who supported just one child in Latin America through an economical sponsorship program ... and ended up changing a life, a family, and sometimes even a community forever!

God doesn't fear numbers. Remember the Apostle Paul said that in our weakness, Christ's strength is perfected! When we feel overwhelmed by the opposition aligned against us, that is exactly when the Lord gives us the power to shine! So it is with Latin America ChildCare. Against all odds, a very personal ministry to the poorest of the poor in the small villages and big slums of Latin America is having an intense impact for the Gospel and in individual lives.

Why? There are many reasons ...

OUR PROGRAM OPENS MINDS. Past president Doug Petersen said it this way:

Latin America ChildCare leads children into a new life by altering their perspectives and attitudes. Many children for the first time see the world from a different angle. They are encouraged to respect their own abilities and opinions, are socialized to feel comfortable in a society with a broader selection of career options, and are equipped with the skills to compete in a competitive job market.

OUR PROGRAM CAN CHANGE ATTITUDES. When children are taught to respect God they can also respect themselves. Selfless commitment to the student's success and compassion for the impoverishment of local citizens are qualities demonstrated daily by national teachers and administrators. These are the types of attitudes that the children come to reflect.

At the same time, the parents of these children are often also affected through a "spill-over effect." When children accept Christ at school, they go home and tell their families about it. Many times, entire families will begin attending church — then be dramatically transformed when they come to faith in Christ!

OUR PROGRAM CAN SAVE LIVES. Our school program seeks to provide many of the children with one full, nourishing meal a day, regular check-ups by doctors and dentists, and whatever medical treatments are necessary.

All these elements are key, because a child entering Latin America ChildCare is probably suffering with low self esteem and a sense of social inferiority. For this affliction, we offer them ... a relationship with God! We teach them ...

> ... that they are made in the image of God.
>
> ... that God loves them.
>
> ... that Jesus Christ, the Son of the Living God, demonstrated the depths of God's compassion in His treatment of the poor and downtrodden, and in His sacrificial death.
>
> ... that the transforming power of Christ over death

itself can surmount even the debilitating effects of poverty,

  ... that their own lives have a purpose, and their souls have an eternal hope!

And these gospel truths create a belief system and an approach that make it possible to continue in the face of some very difficult circumstances:

- The 20 countries that comprise our area of ministry suffer as large a gap between rich and poor as any region of the world.

- And the poor there are poorer than you can imagine.

- Children make up nearly 50 percent of Central America's impoverished people. Life expectancy is low because of lack of clean water and basic health care, plus in some cases, desperately poor nutrition.

Children make up nearly 50% of Central America's impoverished people

Their environment can be largely unstable. Political unrest, as well as natural disasters, such as earthquakes and hurricanes, can cripple a nation and require years of rebuilding efforts.

- At home, children may have to deal with abuse, neglect, alcoholic parents, or families deep in pagan rituals. (That is why we rejoice when we hear testimonies of families transformed by the power of God!)

- So many of these children are doomed. Doomed to hopelessness and poverty without knowing the love of Jesus and His Word.

- Jesus is the only antidote for the pain of the tragic human condition; true hope lies in divine transformation.

So through compassionate aid and educational activities, Latin America ChildCare relies on the faithfulness of God and the supernatural power of the Holy Spirit to supply the needs of the downtrodden and hurting children.

In the pages ahead, you will discover just how powerful that combination can be.

Dick Nicholson

Regional Director
Assemblies of God World Missions
Latin America and the Caribbean

Chairman of the Board
Latin America ChildCare

Introduction

Poverty and despair were stealing away the dreams of the children of El Salvador. Hopelessness leached the spirit of every youngster like a disease. For American-born, Chilean-raised Pastor John Bueno and his wife Lois, seeing the children who lived near their church slowly sucked dry of all self-esteem or hope was heart-rending. It moved them to action.

In 1963, despite the very limited resources of their church, Centro Evangelístico in San Salvador, the missionaries were led to open a small school, combining education with Christian values. This eventually was expanded to include high school and night school.

When Pastor Bueno first shared this plan with the members of Centro Evangelístico, there was little hesitation in the response. Even though, at that time, few members of the congregation owned their own homes and scarcely any had vehicles to drive, they gave from their hearts, and the buildings were built.

This was the genesis of what was to become Latin America ChildCare, built on a vision given by God to one man, and the sacrifice of a single congregation.

God was beginning a miracle.

By 1978, God had called missionaries Doug and Myrna Petersen to service as well, and they began to develop the international focus of LACC. Under their faithful leadership, the successful pattern that had been established in El Salvador was implemented over and over, throughout Latin America.

The plan was two-fold: establishing new churches and schools in slum areas of Latin America cities, and recruiting sponsors for the children.

The gifts of each sponsor would provide a Christian education and things like food, medical care and, in some cases, uniforms for the individual children.

Over the years, God has perfected the first plan into a proven, effective formula of evangelism and education that gives needy children hope. Today, LACC serves some 80,000 children in 300 schools and projects in 20 countries.

LACC is a very cost-effective organization with 85 cents of every sponsorship dollar going directly to meet the needs of the individual child.

It is the loving care, prayer and support of our sponsors that allows us to address a continent of incredible needs, conflict and vast opportunities. Through the leadership of the teachers and administrators in each church and school, and the vision of the many ministry leaders, both international and national, the children are able to grow up knowing God and experiencing His eternal love and care for them.

Certainly, conditions vary from country to country, and sometimes this makes it more difficult to implement the full benefits of the program, but the children enrolled in the LACC-sponsored schools always receive a quality Christ-centered education, and, in most cases, feeding programs and preventative medical care. Each day they learn about Jesus and how He can be their personal Savior!

The children we serve are not just attending classes — they are learning. For instance, in Costa Rica, nearly 100 percent of our students pass the government tests for sixth grade.

And we know that our schools make a huge difference in the lives of the children, and impact their homes and communities. Students take their Bible story lessons home and read them to their parents and siblings. Then perhaps a teacher at the school sponsors an outreach for mothers ... or the parents try attending the affiliated church ... and more lives are saved for Christ! Whole communities are touched — affected in positive ways when families worship together!

Even in the face of physical and emotional suffering, and seemingly insurmountable numbers of children with needs — we must remember that the battle for the souls of the next generation is a spiritual one:

> *For we wrestle not against flesh and blood, but against principalities, against powers, against the rulers of the darkness of this world, against spiritual wickedness in high places. (Ephesians 6:12)*

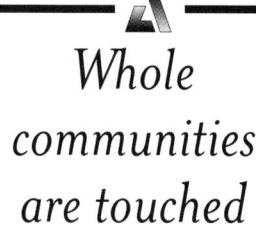

Whole communities are touched

The plan that John Bueno and Doug Petersen initiated and developed for impacting the lives of the children of Latin America is still in place. If you are not familiar with the concept of sponsorship as it applies to LACC, let us tell you what is involved in this vital role of sponsor:

- With a gift of just $28 a month, a compassionate Christian sponsor will provide education and things like food, medical care, and most importantly, an introduction to Jesus.

- The student can be chosen by the sponsor according to age, gender and national origin. Each sponsor will receive a periodic update on his child's progress.

- But beyond that, the sponsors and students are able to write letters throughout the year if they want to — some of the children's letters are especially endearing and encouraging. In addition to that, sponsors also usually send a small financial gift for a Christmas gift. The money is then used to provide a special Christmas celebration and a small gift as the sponsor's present to them.

The children are well aware the difference a sponsorship provides them. They understand that the sponsors are Christians, who want to help needy children because of the example of Christ. The children are grateful — to be sure. But also they experience increased self-worth and security, because someone cares enough for them to make sure they get food, an education, medical care, and a chance to grow in their faith.

Prayer is a crucial part of the sponsorship commitment. The children are not only impacted by financial giving, but also by the covenant to pray for the child. We believe that the prayer commitment is as important as the financial one, impacting that life regardless of the miles between.

Sponsorship is not like adoption. Most of these children live in homes with at least one of their parents. But often the sponsors and students begin to think of one another as extended family because the bonds grow strong over the years.

All of the children that are available for sponsorship in the LACC program come from needy areas. Many of their parents are unemployed or severely underemployed. Many children suffer from malnutrition. They care for younger siblings, or work as street vendors to help support their families.

Sponsorship saves a child's life ... sometimes literally as well as spiritually.

Sometimes caring Christians become sponsors of multiple children. Their "family" grows with the addition of another sponsored child or children. That means LOTS of love and letters coming and going through the mail, and daily prayer and monthly gifts to help to ensure the education and spiritual growth of the children.

It is our view that healthy, productive adults don't just happen — they're built. But in the crushing poverty of Latin America and the Caribbean, that building process can be difficult. LACC provides each child with the building blocks: a good education, an opportunity to live in Christ, and things like health and nutrition.

These things are all that is needed for a child to escape from the cycle of poverty, and become leaders and pillars of their own communities. To become productive workers and responsible parents. And to live out the dreams that they have dared to dream during their youth at an LACC school!

Latin America ChildCare is a God-birthed ministry. Our success stories are evidence of God at work in young people who have broken out of poverty and hopelessness. Those who find hope and comfort in the arms of the Living God. And those who turn around when they are grown, becoming teachers, staff and administrators of LACC-sponsored schools and churches in their own communities.

Our successes are measured by those who have shared Christ with their parents and siblings, bringing salvation to their own homes.

The students of LACC-sponsored schools are impacting their communities for Christ, and as they grow, they are ultimately beginning to change the face of their home nations.

We would like to share with you what God has done so far through this ministry. I know you will be blessed by this compilation of stories gathered throughout our many years of service in Latin America and the Caribbean from teachers, sponsors — and even students themselves.

What you will read here is not fiction. These are stories that evidence the love of God among us, His compassion, direction and leading ... and His perfect plan for each believer.

As you enjoy the memories we share of our joys and pain, illustrating the incomparable value of Latin America ChildCare in the lives of the children ...

> ... please be aware that there are thousands of children waiting and praying for sponsors at this moment. Children who long for the security and personal value that comes from a sponsor's love and commitment.

If you are already a sponsor, then we invite you to — in the words of one LACC graduate — "Just look around and see what God has done!"

The stories in the pages of this book come from all eras and all nations of the Latin America ChildCare ministry, so they are not in chronological or geographical order, so the circumstances may have changed since the telling ... but you can be assured that each story points out the radical difference God's love can make and has made, administered through compassionate friends like you.

Ken Dahlager
Steve Alsup

Directors
Latin America ChildCare

CHAPTER ONE
Changed by Salvation
Love and Persistence in the Barrios of Guatemala

Carlos knew right from wrong, and he knew the life he was living was wrong. But the addiction to alcohol is a tough one to beat — and when he was sober, Carlos had to face head-on the reality that he was too poor to provide anything but the most meager shelter and support for his family. He had to face the reality that his little children would never have a brighter future. It was much easier just to stay lost in a alcoholic haze.

He surfaced from time to time and made a show of changing. He spent several days working side-by-side with a volunteer construction team from Canada, building a new school for the children in his community. In fact, he stayed sober during this time and came to really enjoy the work and sharing with the members of the team. One of them led Carlos to Christ, and another offered to sponsor Carlos' eldest child to attend the new school!

It was a chance at a new beginning, but Carlos stumbled. He never enrolled his children in the new school ... and he couldn't fight off the need for alcohol for long. When one of our missionaries came to check on Carlos and his family, they found his despairing wife alone with the four hungry children in their 5 X 10 bamboo hut ... and Carlos was out spending their meager week's income on a drinking binge.

Missionaries Cary Goshinmon and Alan Slater were heartbroken to learn about Carlo's relapse, but they determined to help his children, anyway. They committed to sponsor two of the three school-aged children themselves, so they could all be enrolled in school, and then they even made special arrangements with the school director for a special feeding program to meet the children's lagging nutritional needs and build their strength.

The children were overjoyed; their faces lit up with the promise of food and care at the new school.

For the first couple years, all went well. Last year, times got too tough for Carlos and his family, and they decided to make ends meet, their oldest child at least would have to go to work. This year, none of the children are in school. Please pray that God will provide a way to bring them back into the fold.

God's Word Comes Into a Home

In Haiti, voodoo is a way of life with an entrenched history and a demonic power that oppresses hundreds of thousands. It was no different in Endreneme's neighborhood ... but Endreneme was different.

Her parents had raised her and her brothers and sisters to believe that Jesus saves! The entire family faithfully attended the Assemblies of God church next to the school sponsored by LACC.

Endreneme, or Endre for short, was "12 years old," and had never attended school. The family was much too poor to send Endre or her six little brothers to school. They would have very much liked to have educated their children, particularly because none of them could read much, and they had never been able to read the Word of God in their own home.

When the school director gave Endre the good news that a sponsor had been found for her, the little girl was overjoyed, and made up her mind to be a hard-working student. Since then, several of her younger brothers have been sponsored too, and every one of them is excelling.

Endre may be only 12 years old but she plays a significant role in changing her family's future because — Endre has learned to read! Every night after the evening meal she reads Scripture to her parents and brothers. She says,

> *I love the school and my teachers. I see the love of Jesus in them and they really care for me. They not only teach me how to read, but they have given me a deeper respect for God, my elders and a hope for the future.*
>
> *I want to marry and have a family of my own. I am going to teach my children to love God and respect their elders.*

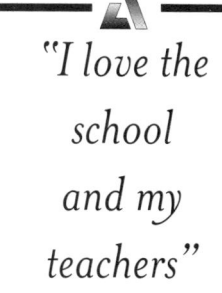

"*I love the school and my teachers*"

Endre thinks life without the church and the LACC-sponsored school would have been grim and hopeless.

> *I would have been worshipping Satan like so many of my friends in the neighborhood. I pray to God and ask Him to bless my sponsors. Without their help, I don't know where my life would have gone.*

The lives of Endre, her siblings and her parents have all been dramatically changed in eternal ways because of the unselfish love shown by compassionate sponsors thousands of miles away.

Trading Gang Life — For Life in Christ

At 13, Ovidio was already a member of a violent and dangerous gang, and a discipline problem at home.

Although his parents were Jehovah's Witnesses, they agreed to send him to an LACC-sponsored school hoping that our reputation for changing children's lives could be true for their son, too.

We hoped for a rapid victory as Ovidio attended religious education classes with the other children and seemed to understand the Gospel. Officially the lad professed "no interest in changing religions," and remained "tight" with his gang.

The gang, having seen a dramatization of "the perfect crime" on television, decided they would try it for themselves. So they broke into a bicycle store, tied up the young lady who worked there and threw her on the floor, then stole as much money and merchandise as they could carry.

Of course, there was nothing perfect about their crime and they were all arrested almost immediately, still possessing all the evidence.

Not really as tough as the image he projected, Ovidio was terrified when he was handcuffed and taken to "a real horrible prison."

Thankfully, the judge in Ovidio's case had heard about Latin America ChildCare and the good work we're doing in the lives of poor children, by introducing them to, and helping them grow in Christ.

At the judge's suggestion, the school director agreed to have the boy released into our custody. After that, things began to change. Ovidio immediately resigned from his gang.

One morning in a chapel service, Ovidio felt that something extraordinary was happening to him during a message on repentance. Tears began to flow down his face, and he testified that in that moment, "Jesus changed my life. Jesus has forgiven my sins."

Still awaiting trial, it is unclear what his future will be, but Ovidio has a changed life and now speaks with true bravery:

> I don't know what will happen to me, but I am no longer afraid. I have a favorite verse which comforts me from Isaiah 43:1, 'Don't be afraid because I have redeemed you. I have called you by my name and you are mine.'

Two Final Wishes

Yair Ulises Uribe Velasquez was about to finish the third grade at his LACC-sponsored school, Centro Educativo Candelaria in Mexico City. Then with just a few weeks to go, he inexplicably quit attending classes!

In Latin America, it is not uncommon for impoverished families to move frequently. They may hear of a job opportunity in a different city, or be forced to move in with relatives in another part of town ... Yair's teachers wondered if perhaps his family had suddenly relocated.

But then as summer vacation began, Yair returned. He wanted to be sure he could come back to school for the next academic year. Missionary Eva Valdez enthusiastically agreed and, a few days later, Yair's parents registered him for school ... but they seemed terribly unhappy ... and eventually they told Eva why.

Their son had only two or three months left to live

Yair had missed the final few weeks of school because he had been hospitalized with leukemia. The doctors said their son had only two or three months left to live, and they did not want him to spend his precious last days attending school. But Yair saw it differently. He was determined to learn more about his Savior Jesus before they met face to face.

A few days later, Yair visited Ms. Valdez again. He explained to her his two wishes — to have his parents know Jesus, and to attend the school's Kids Camp, still seven months away. What could he do about it? With Ms. Valdez's encouragement, Yair began to pray day and night, often visiting with the missionary so they could pray together ... and miraculously, he was able to attend camp with the other kids!

On the bus ride home from camp, Yair came to sit with Ms. Valdez. "Miss Eva," he said, "I'm ready."

"Oh?" she replied. "Ready to join the soccer team, or what?"

Yair took a deep breath. "Miss Eva," he said again, "I'm ready."

"Miss Eva" — or Ms. Valdez — suddenly understood. "That's right, Yair," she said, placing her hand over his heart and fighting the lump in her throat, "you just keep Jesus right there in your heart."

A few days later, Yair was hospitalized again and he asked Ms. Valdez to visit him. He only said, "My mom, my dad," when she came in, but she understood. She went to present the Gospel to Mr. and Mrs. Uribe ... who welcomed Jesus into their hearts! *God had answered both of Yair's fervent prayer requests.*

The young boy died that night ... and went to his Father's eternal home to finally meet Jesus.

At the end of the school year, the school invited Yair's parents to receive, on his behalf, the beautiful plaque and leather Bible given to all graduates, so Yair's baby brother — only a few months old when Yair died — could learn about Jesus like Yair did.

Yair's sponsorship has made an eternal impact.

Teaching for Moms

Liceo Christiano Bethesda School, located in a poor barrio outside Guatemala City, Guatemala, has few modern conveniences. The space is cramped and there is no running water.

But the teachers there are a marvel of sacrifice and dedication. Each one works a double session, teaching the school's 1,350 students, from kindergarten to high school.

As the school director, Ernestina Saso also balances her extensive administrative duties with the responsibilities of teaching a Sunday School class and also her own unique outreach to the mothers of her students.

For over 10 years, she has led a Sunday forum where 40-50 local women come together to discuss the things of the Lord. In Ernestina's fellowship, no one is allowed to just listen. The women are not only expected to participate — but each of them is required to lead the discussion at least once.

The children thoroughly enjoy seeing their mothers and the other women bringing home lesson plans and assignments!

"Many times, the mothers aren't Christians," Ernestina says. "They are single or live with husbands who are addicted to drugs or alcohol, or abusive. They need this class to hear the Word."

Another teacher whose ministry reaches mothers is Sonia Waleska Diaz of San Pedro Sula, Honduras. Sonia has the pleasure of making her impact for Christ in Escuela Evangelica Beracah, the same LACC-sponsored school that she first came to as a fifth grade student in 1983.

> *When I entered this school, I began to learn about the Word of the Lord through my Bible class and devotions. I was slowly beginning to feel the need to give my life to the Lord.*

Sonia has not only made that vital decision for Christ, she came to another conclusion as well. She says,

> *I wanted to be a teacher, and work in the same institution where my life was changed. To give the best of my abilities, intellectually and spiritually, to these students, year after year, so they will continue to come.*

For teachers like Ernestina and Sonia, the long classroom hours are just the beginning of their commitment. Both take on extra church responsibilities like visits to children's homes and community service projects. For them, and hundreds like them in Latin America ChildCare, teaching isn't a job — it's a committed lifestyle.

Enrique

Enrique was young and energetic. He attended school during the day, then in the evenings he worked to help support his family. He cleaned tables at a local restaurant — and no matter how late the work kept him up in the evenings, he was always on time for school the next day, bright and eager to learn.

One day, several weeks ago, Enrique was one of the last students to finish writing a letter to his sponsor. He labored to make it perfect and included his favorite scripture verse. Sister Bojorquez (school director of the Campestre's school in El Salvador) waited patiently as Enrique worked diligently to capture his thoughts on the page. Here is what he wrote to his North American sponsors ...

> *It's a joy to be able to greet you through this letter. Thank you for writing me ... your words encourage me and give me strength, as we serve the same God.*
>
> *It is very important to keep a close fellowship with God ... I thank and praise God because He helps me do well in my job. In the book of Revelation, chapter 2, verse 10, it reads:*
>
> *"Fear none of those things which thou shalt suffer: behold, the devil shall cast some of you into prison, that you may be tried; and ye shall have tribulation ten days: be thou faithful unto death, and I will give thee a crown of life."*
>
> *I'll say goodbye to you in the name of the Lord. May the Lord God greatly bless you.*
>
> *Enrique Geovanni Estrada Lopez.*

As soon as he finished his note, he hurried home so he could catch a nap before he had to go to work that night. When his grandma came to wake him up to go to his job, she found that Enrique's heart had stopped while he slept, and he had gone into the presence of the Lord.

Although he is sorely missed by his family and friends, they know that he had been "faithful unto death" and has received the crown of life in eternity with Christ.

A Child Gives the Gift of Christ

When a missionary woman came to share the Gospel at their house, Natali was a very young girl. Everyone listened, but only the children believed. Natali and her brothers and sisters accepted Christ into their hearts — and her parents did not. Meanwhile, God was at work in the lives of these children, as completion was nearing on a new school for Latin America ChildCare. God had a plan for Natali, who had been attending public school, but then became enrolled to begin second grade at the new school.

Natali is older now, and very expressive. She has no trouble relaying the truth of God's grace to her:

> *Ever since this time, my life has changed in such a special way. I received a Christian education and lessons, and everything I learned, I shared with my mother.*

This sweet child, even at her tender age, made an impact for Christ by bringing home her Christian education books for her mother to read. One day Natali received joyous news when her mother told her that she wanted to go to church. During the service, her mother, too, finally accepted Christ.

A cheerful testimony to the power of God is the healing of Natali's older sister who has suffered terribly from asthma for years, but Natali says,

> *The Lord has healed her, and now we are a very happy family. We can now say thank you to the Lord for this Christian school, one which has been a great blessing for many children in the community, for this has been a light in the midst of darkness.*

Today, Natali is involved in her church's mime ministry and

mission group — and is keenly aware of the impact that the gifts of Christians, thousands of miles away, have made in her life. The testimony of this young lady is clear:

> *Who I am today, I owe all to Jesus who demonstrates His love through the help of my sponsors.*

"God ... If You're Real..."

Dulce (whose name means "sweet") grew up with four brothers and sisters in the poorest barrio town of the Dominican Republic.

Her mother had a live-in boyfriend who became violent and abusive. One day, nine-year-old Dulce prayed to a God she did not know:

"If you are real, all I want is peace in our home!"

Soon afterward, the boyfriend left!

Dulce's mother moved the family to an abandoned house with a leaky roof. She struggled daily to sell enough candy on the streets to buy food for her children. As a result, Dulce became relegated to the overwhelming position of substitute mother in her house.

> *"God, if you are real, all I want is to go to school"*

One day while sweeping, the desperate little girl decided to ask the unknown God for one more thing:

"God, if you are real, all I want is to go to school."

Not long after, some women from a local Assemblies of God church invited Dulce and her mother to a Saturday night women's revival service. Both accepted Christ that evening, and the next morning when Dulce's brothers were given the opportunity to meet Christ — they were saved too!

That same Sunday afternoon, the pastor came to visit ... and offered to sponsor the children in the church's Latin America ChildCare school.

By Monday morning, not just Dulce, but her brothers too, were in classrooms, wearing new uniforms, enjoying a nutritious lunch, and meeting their new Christian teacher. They were discovering real hope for the first time in their lives.

And Dulce knew that this was a mighty answer to her tiny prayer.

The children's mother was so overwhelmed with gratitude that she volunteered to clean the school in the late afternoons. Soon the school was able to pay her for her labor. Then a widowed deacon who came out from the church to repair her roof was so impressed with this mother's character that he eventually became Dulce's stepfather.

Ultimately, Dulce and her family came to live in a fine middle-class home of sturdy adobe, filled with peace and love.

"Look around," Dulce said. "See what God has done."

Time slipped by. Not long ago on a visit to the Latin America ChildCare school that had educated Dulce, one of our workers went into the office to inquire about some unsponsored youngsters, and who should look up to greet him? The secretary ... Dulce!

Now happily married, she is juggling studies at the university with work at her old school ... where her pastor says her sensitivity and compassion are a blessing to all the children.

So a divine plan makes a full circle.

A young girl's desperate cry to an unknown God led to His blessing and the unfolding of His superior plan for her life. And now, in appreciation, Dulce chooses to invest her changed life in relieving the desperation of other impoverished children.

An Intersection on the Road to Hell

Jorge's dad died when he was 11 days old. His mother, working as a cashier in a local restaurant, felt she couldn't afford to keep him so she left him with his grandmother and aunts when he was four months old. The result was not good. At a very tender age, Jorge began running the streets, staying out all night, smoking, and running with a gang. At eleven years of age, he was already lost.

But Jesus had another plan for him, and Jorge tells it in his own words:

> One night, I had just returned from running with my friends and had just laid down, when I started dreaming. I fell into a deep sleep as if it were 5 AM in the morning. In my mind, I saw a long road with thousands of people walking on it.
>
> I came close to an intersection that was covered with fog. In the middle of the intersection, I saw Jesus. Jesus' face was shining like the sun. Jesus was standing in front of the way that He wanted everyone to take. It was a beautiful road. When I got to the intersection, Jesus pointed to a dark road indicating I was to take that road. I started to cry bitterly. I turned back to Jesus to see if He would forgive me, but He was still pointing to the dark road.
>
> I finally got to the end of that road and there was such a large dark pit that I couldn't see the other side. All of a sudden, I saw the flames of a fire that looked like the eruption of a volcano coming from the pit. I knew that was hell and hell was waiting for me! I ran back to Jesus and threw myself at His feet saying, "Lord, forgive me and give me another chance!" Jesus said to me, "I will give you another chance but this is your last chance! You are to serve me and win others for me!"

Jesus showed me that time was short and I needed to tell others about Him. I thank God that He has given me a gift to preach His word and give others the opportunity to know Him.

Now a student at Escuela Rosa De Saron in Nicaragua, Jorge became a Christian because of an unusual — even radical — conversion. But the evidence of his calling is unmistakable.

During Easter week, Jorge and two of his Christian friends preached on the street to a large crowd of people. According to his grandmother, 50-60 young children accepted Christ during the altar call. Jorge is now teaching other children and helping the pastor.

Jorge hasn't decided what he wants to do with his life, but he knows one thing for sure — he never wants to live without Jesus again.

King of the Street Gangs

Alex Villalta Moroe was incorrigible.

He had been expelled from public school and put in the juvenile detention center because of his violent attacks upon other students. This pleased him, because now he could hang out on the streets with his gang — full-time.

Even the older street thugs feared Alex. Belying his youth, his quick temper and skill with a knife were well documented. He spent most of his days robbing people and then partying on the stolen money. Once in a while he would return to his home in Torremolinos, where his father made a living as a drug dealer.

Arriving home triggered familiar patterns. Alex's father would threaten him and force him to sell drugs for him. Eventually his father would beat him up badly and Alexander would return to the streets.

Torremolinos is a community known for its drug trade, gangs and difficult living conditions. It's no wonder that everyone was shocked when Latin America ChildCare opened a school right in the middle of Torremolinos — a school where children could learn, regardless of background or what their dad did for a living.

Alex was certainly not an ideal candidate for Christian school. Amazingly, his father enrolled him and forced him to attend. The boy's violent behavior quickly landed him in the director's office — where he assumed he would be beaten as he had been in the public school.

Instead, school director Patricia Sandoval talked to Alex about his life and his family. Alexander found her interest intriguing, yet he also found it hard to believe that she really cared about him.

Patricia invited Alex's father to come and talk too, and for the first time the two were able to express things to each other that they had never even dreamed of saying in their home.

It was as if the walls between the father and child were tumbling down!

As the director of the school, Patricia felt that she had to suspend Alexander, for the protection of the other students. But she promised if he proved he could control his temper and leave his knife at home, he could come back.

For days, Alex waited near the school, hoping to catch a glimpse of his teachers and friends. The care and concern he received from the teachers didn't make sense. He had never even wanted to go to school before, and now he couldn't get back in if he wanted to … Alex fingered his knife and wondered if it wouldn't be easier to simply end his own misery right then.

Yet something deep inside the boy would not allow him to commit suicide. He went to talk with Patricia. She still wouldn't let him return to school, but she agreed to allow him on the school field trip, as long as he brought no weapons or drugs.

Students would spend a weekend at the "King's Castle" children's evangelism camp. Patricia explained to Santiago Loacigia, the full-time program leader, that Alex would come. That weekend, puppets, games, singing and all the activities emphasized God's love.

One night as Santiago gave the invitation for children to accept Christ, Alex walked forward to pray. It was as if every person present held their breath — could this really be Alex, the king of the street gangs?

But Alex prayed with Santiago, then Patricia, then other LACC teachers and even the students. It was a true salvation, a total surrender of the heart — and Alex would never be the same!

Today, Alex is 24 years old, a graduate from the LACC program, and working as a pastry chef at the Hotel Costa Rica. He's been married to Yeimy for five years and they have a beautiful four-year-old daughter, Fabiola.

Alex would never be the same!

Alex and his wife, Yeimy attend the Crusade of Faith church in Desamparados and they are very excited about serving Jesus. He said they have had difficult times in their marriage when they wanted to separate, but counseling and the Word of God have kept them together. They are committed to growing in Christ and raising Fabiola in a godly home. Their daughter sometimes says things that surprise them with what she has learned from the Bible!

Alex still remembers the advice that Patricia, the Torremolinos principal, gave him when he was involved with gangs and drugs and was so hot-tempered. She said "a real man knows when to stay quiet and choose his words carefully, when to forgive someone, and when to ask forgiveness." That advice has stuck with him, and has helped him to keep his cool and avoid arguments.

Forbid Them Not

After being hospitalized for 20 days when she was a tiny infant in her home town of Lima, Peru, Marisol was released to her mother with tragic news: the baby was HIV positive.

Marisol's father, an officer in the Peruvian Navy, had unknowingly infected his wife with HIV, and she had passed it on to their baby.

Still Marisol was not in immediate danger for her life. She did not develop AIDS, and was soon old enough for school.

But the public school in her Lima neighborhood would not accept her. They claimed she was a danger to the other children and teachers because of her disease.

Her mother hoped for the best for her little girl and wanted Marisol to receive an education, so she went to another school in their poor neighborhood: the "Jesus Is Lord" school associated with Latin America ChildCare.

Pastor David Pariasca gathered the teachers and staff together to discuss the issue. They remembered the words of Jesus who said:

> *Suffer the little children to come unto me, and forbid them not: for of such is the kingdom of God. (Mark 10:14)*

They agreed to trust Jesus to protect them and the other children from the AIDS virus. After that, Marisol attended the "Jesus Is Lord" school for a year — and what a year it was!

Marisol learned about Jesus and made a commitment to live for Him. Her mother and dad also came to know the Lord through the ministry of the school.

Ultimately her father developed AIDS and died, but they knew he was in heaven and that helped their pain. Then Marisol succumbed to the illness ... and finally her mother.

As sad as this story is, it could have been much sadder. Marisol might never have known Jesus as Lord and Savior ... might never have even known human acceptance, had she not come to the LACC-sponsored school. If that had not happened of course, her parents might not have found their salvation in Christ either.

Pastor Pariasca says:

> *We thank God for each person who decides to sponsor a child they may never meet. God in His infinite mercy extends His*

hands to these children through these generous brothers and sisters who feel God's love for the children.

One Life Changed Forever

It would be hard to come from a poorer neighborhood than Luis did.

He was just six when he first began attending the Latin America ChildCare-sponsored school in the community of Linda Vista, a poor area of the larger region of Desamparados, outside San Jose, Costa Rica — and one of the worst of all the slums Latin America ChildCare worked in at the time.

Luis' family's house was in terrible condition, a ramshackle combination of tin walls and black cardboard roof.

And his family life wasn't much better than his house.

Neither of his parents were Christians. His clothes were little better than rags, his hand-me-down boots doing little to keep out the cold and damp.

"I remember vividly the day the director of the school, Mr. Mario Camacho, gave me a new pair of shoes," Luis says. He remembers other things too. "A lot of times, the only food I would get during the day was the meal I received at school."

Luis' third grade teacher led him to Christ one March day, which he now calls, "the most meaningful and life-changing moment in my life. My teacher gave me the invitation to turn my life over to Jesus. I did it only once and for the rest of my life.

> *I am so thankful to God for the church-school relationship that existed at that time, because it gave me the opportunity to grow in Christ and it allowed God to mold and direct my life according to His will.*
>
> *When I was 10 years old, during a worship service, God*

spoke to my heart telling me that I would one day be His servant. [This event] changed my life and planted a strong desire in me to serve Him with my whole being.

A year later, Luis — just 11 years old — won a "King's Castle" Bible verse competition ... and even found himself preaching to his congregation.

The desire to share what he was learning with others grew strong in Luis. His family eventually moved to a nearby slum area so that their son could attend the Latin America ChildCare-sponsored high school in that community.

Luis grew more and more involved in his local Assemblies of God church. After graduating from high school, he attended a university and later, an Assemblies of God Bible school.

He is now a teacher himself in one of our Latin America ChildCare-sponsored schools ... as well as youth pastor and head of his church's Sunday school program. He hopes "in God's time" to become a pastor.

I give thanks to the Lord that there once was a school that took me in and taught me about God. I now am able to sponsor a child and instill in many children biblical principles.

Thanks be to the Lord, for the church-school design, which has allowed me to be and grow as God's servant.

CHAPTER TWO

Changed by Healing
Ready or Not!

He could hear the friend who was counting and he was running out of time: "Eight, nine, ten – ready or not, here I come."

Hide-And-Go-Seek is daily fare on the playground at a certain LACC-sponsored school in Santo Domingo. But this day when his time to hide was running out, Ronnie Fernandez Breton made a desperate dive for a hideaway, without considering the fact that he was on the second floor. Ronnie accidentally fell two stories to the ground!

His frightened classmates and teachers rushed to him and began to pray, even as they called for medical help.

The doctors were not hopeful. After such a serious fall, and considering the extent of his internal injuries, Ronnie was not expected to recover.

But his teachers and friends refused to accept the diagnosis! The children, teachers, and staff prayed for Ronnie daily, visiting him in the hospital and later at home. And when Ronnie not only lived, but began to recover, the doctors and medical caregivers were absolutely astounded!

Before long his teacher started coming to the house from his school each day to catch him up in his schoolwork, with every expectation that he would return to his desk in the classroom shortly.

And she was right! Ronnie was totally healed by God's power!

Our little student's mind and body were completely restored, and he returned to himself fully, and is now a healthy, rambunctious little boy once more.

Only God Could Free Him

Young Daniel Armando came to us after two years in public school where he had learned — almost nothing.

The public school couldn't offer much of an education to his impoverished neighborhood. But we know they did try to help him, even sending him to the school therapist. When he had first started at the public school, Daniel's mother, Isabelle, had high hopes that school would change things, but nothing helped.

Isabelle had high hopes that school would change things, but nothing helped

The problem seemed to be that Daniel was unable to learn. His mother didn't think she would ever see him function as a completely normal child. Isabelle says, "Daniel had severe problems all his life. He didn't want to speak with anyone, and he never played with the other children. At night, he awakened crying, terrorized or screaming from nightmares."

By the end of his second year of school, Daniel could still not write his name or count. His teacher said she had never even heard the sound of Daniel's voice. A desperate Isabelle brought her son to the Latin America ChildCare school in their neighborhood.

Almost immediately, the boy's outlook and behavior began to change.

Daniel accepted Christ as Savior. His nightmares disappeared completely. He learned to read, write and count, and Daniel's teachers were able to prepare him academically and spiritually.

"Soon everything he had suffered was in his past, and the Lord Jesus Christ had healed every area of his life," Isabelle declares.

"My son knew that God was the only one who could free him from all his oppression. Hallelujah!"

A Doctor Brings Comfort and Healing

Santa Cruz del Quiché, a poor town in Guatemala, joyfully welcomed a Latin America ChildCare missionary team from First Assembly of Ft. Collins, Colorado.

An eye doctor and two general practitioners were soon absorbed with relieving the suffering of families who have little access to medical care otherwise. One baby was saved from certain blindness — just because she was able to receive the most basic of medications that the staff brought with them.

But for Gwen Kovac, a missionary working with Latin America ChildCare in Guatemala at the time, the presence of a volunteer chiropractor was perplexing. Never one to turn away volunteer medical assistance, Gwen was hard pressed to imagine what valuable contribution he might make.

But God was about to reveal His plan.

It is the custom of Guatemalan ladies — and the men too, sometimes — to carry large bundles balanced on their heads. It's not hard to imagine that a woman who carries a 50-pound load on top of her head might experience neck and back trouble — as well as headaches.

And then there are the ladies who kneel before their looms,

weaving eight hours a day — who experience muscle pain, cramps, callused ankles and knees ...

... so when word got out that Dr. Carr specialized in these problems, he immediately became the most popular man in the village!

Starting at 8 AM every day, he eased muscle pain and severe headaches, adjusted backs and necks — and worked all day, only to finish examinations by flashlight after the sun went down!

Surprised and grateful, his patients spread the word about Dr. Carr's ministry of comfort and healing, until finally little Dina Ester was brought to him.

One of the child's feet turned sharply inward, pointing in towards the other foot. She had never been able to walk normally — and running had always been out of the question.

In order to help her, the doctor would have to fit the bones and muscles back into their proper places.

"Actually, it frightened us to hear how those little bones would crack as Dr. Carr placed his tender, healing hands on Dina's legs. You could hear the bones as they were being put into place," Gwen said. "But God's plan was fulfilled and today Dina runs and walks as normally as any other seven-year-old-girl!"

The Guatemalan missionaries and the citizens of Santa Cruz del Quiché have grateful hearts and appreciate the many who have donated time and funding for these medical missions.

"God Is Confusing Me"

Sotela had cause to be bewildered as she poured her heart out to her good friend Mary, the LACC regional coordinator. A recent widow with two young daughters, Gabriella, 5 and Genesis, 3, Sotela had been looking for work in their town of El Pauji, near Caracas, Venezuela, for months.

Just a week after she had finally landed a job, she began to notice mysterious bruises appearing all over Gabriella.

She took Gaby to the doctor, who diagnosed her as having Purpura Syndrome, an illness that causes the patient's blood platelets, normally at a count of 250,000, to be much lower. Gaby's count was 33,000. The doctor prescribed a rigorous treatment of steroids, vitamins, and diet restrictions. The mother had no choice but to comply, or lose her daughter.

So every Monday morning at 4:30 AM, Sotela would travel with Gaby to the doctor, and the entire day would be spent having medical tests done. Each time she would pray that Gaby's platelets might have risen to at least 175,000. Each time, the results stubbornly came back at just 33,000.

Of course, Sotela's new boss grew irritated with her Monday absences, and fired her. She was back to where she started, with no income, only now she had a very sick child. She couldn't help wondering what more God could expect from her.

But she still had a church, and she faithfully took Gaby and Genesis to the Fuente de Vida church to worship and pray for a healing.

One Sunday evening, Byron Klaus, who at the time was Vice President of Latin America ChildCare, was preaching. Afterward he invited people forward for prayer and Sotela wasted no time in bringing Gaby to the front. Byron prayed and laid hands on her, and Sotela went home that evening with hope in her heart.

This time, Sotela did not awake to her usual Monday morning dread. She really sensed that God was going to heal her little girl. Eagerly she awaited test results that had always before yielded the same bad news. She dared to believe that the platelet count might have even doubled!

But when the test results came back this time, they showed a platelet count over 300,000 — a number comfortably above normal! There was no doubt that God had thoroughly healed this little girl of a deadly blood disorder!

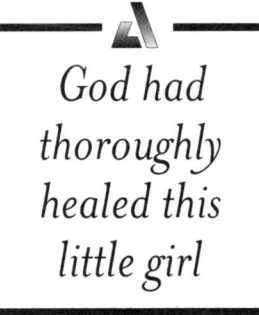

God had thoroughly healed this little girl

Now Gabriella not only has the hope of a long, healthy life, but thanks to Sotela's good friend, Mary, Gaby will have a more meaningful life as well. Mary has decided to sponsor Gaby as a student at the communities new LACC-sponsored school.

Whatever "confusion" Sotela may still have, she is now certain that God hears her prayers, and that He has a loving, nurturing plan for her family!

"He Never Left Me"

Torremolinos, a barrio in the southern portion of San Jose, Costa Rica, is a very dangerous place, known for drugs and gang members that are armed to the teeth.

On a warm April night in that neighborhood, Wendy, a 10-year-old student at our Torremolinos school was at her kitchen table, putting the finishing touches on her homework. Her 16-year-old brother Jose came in carrying a gun he had found by the river. No one knows why the .36 caliber Smith and Wesson revolver was left there.

Another brother, Edgar, was fixing himself something to eat in the kitchen and Jose called him over to "see something." From this point on, an ominous situation became the worst nightmare possible. Edgar recalls:

> *Jose called me over to see his gun, but while I was walking toward him, the gun accidentally went off. I saw my little sister falling off the chair and lots of blood started coming out of her head. I took her in my arms and asked her not to go to sleep.*

"My God will not take me away, will He?" asked little Wendy. She cried out to God and pleaded for Jesus not to take her away, because she wanted to live. Then she fainted in her brother's arms. Edgar began to scream for help.

Later, in the intensive care unit of a local hospital, Wendy fell into a coma and doctors believed there was no way for Wendy to survive the accident, because the bullet had traveled all the way through the side of her head. If she did live, the doctors assured the family she would be left a "vegetable" her entire life. Even the local newspaper reported that she had little chance of survival.

Wendy's mother prayed. Wendy's teachers prayed. Wendy's classmates prayed.

Then a miracle occurred. Wendy recalls:

> *I woke up at the hospital. The first time I did was to pinch myself to see if it all was a nightmare, or if it was real. I told my mother I thanked God because this accident was going to be a testimony to my brothers to change their lifestyle and leave those scary gangs.*

Every night, Wendy prayed and asked for God to keep her alive and allow her to come back home — walking on her own two feet — so she could see her family and friends at her school. Wendy tells us,

> *The Lord did something amazing in my life. The first time when I saw Jose, my brother, I hugged him and cried with him, because I was so happy to be alive. I could not hold any anger in my heart, because I knew that God took care of me even during this horrible accident.*
>
> *Now I know there is a God who cares for His little ones, like me. He has many people to take care of and they are constantly asking for help. But HE NEVER LEFT ME ALONE!*

Wendy attends the LACC-sponsored school in Torremolinos. Like all students she receives a Christian education, and things like a nutritious meal and medical assistance there.

But what saved her life that night in April was her personal faith in Jesus and her belief in His promises.

In our Latin America ChildCare classrooms, we teach the children that the Lord hears our cries. We know when Wendy cried out in her simple child-like faith, God heard the little girl's prayers … and He kept her alive. Because the Word says:

> *The eyes of the Lord are upon the righteous, and His ears are open unto their cry* (Psalm 34:15).

"He Scared the Devil Out of Me"

It is the friends and supporters of Latin America ChildCare that make it possible for us to provide the boys and girls with quality education, but it is the transforming power of God that truly makes the difference in their lives, as Johnny Esquivel can tell you.

Johnny is the national LACC director for Costa Rica. He is an insightful man, sensitive to the leading of God and — foremost in his heart — he is a servant to children.

When the principal of one of the schools he administers became seriously ill, Johnny spent a week substituting as the principal in his place.

During the week, a child was sent to the principal's office, carrying with him the teacher's strong recommendation that he should be expelled!

A note like that comes as something of a shock, since LACC-sponsored schools exist to serve the children, and few are ever entirely kicked out of school.

What's more, the teachers who work in these classrooms are devoted, unselfish people. They are universally patient, love the Lord, and are terrific conduits of God's love to their students every day.

So when this request came saying that this child was too disruptive and aggressive to stay in school, Johnny knew he had a very serious situation on his hands.

The boy was out of control.

When Johnny tried to speak with him about his behavior, the little fellow was unresponsive and resistant to every suggestion that Johnny made.

Sighing, Johnny gently asked if he could pray for the boy, and the student agreed to allow this ...

... and the power of God simply fell all over the child as Johnny prayed!

It was a transforming moment that shaped a little boy's entire life! He returned to class — not only still enrolled — but a completely changed child!

His teacher and the rest of the school staff were shocked. All of the students that he had tormented were amazed. This young man had been a problem ever since he started attending classes, and then the bad behavior just suddenly ... stopped.

A day or two later, his teacher asked him, "What did Johnny do to you?"

"He scared the devil out of me," declared the former troublemaker.

But we know that Johnny didn't scare the devil out of the boy — the Lord Jesus Christ did that Himself. That our God continues to do mighty things for us is a reality we try to share at our schools every day.

As God redeems the next generation in Latin America and prepares them for His service, we rejoice in the supernatural, instantaneous transforming power of our God!

A Timid Child

Jayar Thomas has a learning disability as well as emotional and developmental problems. When his mother, Claudette, first registered him to attend classes at our Harvest Hill school in

Botany Bay, Jamaica, he hated and feared it.

Every day, Claudette had to pry his hands loose from her just to turn him over to this teacher, and then Jayar would continue to cry for a couple more hours ... every day. He has been in the first grade class for two years now. A decision to hold Jayar back has proved a good one — with patient guidance he has experienced a lot of healing and has started to participate.

> "Jayar is just one of the many little lives I have seen changed"

Claudette says that he was once rude and angry at home and she had a hard time handling him. But now she can see a significant improvement in his attitude. Though Jayar still has problems — like being timid and shy at school — he is making definite progress. There is a tremendous healing taking place in his classroom.

Jayar's teacher, Mrs. Marion Steward Williams, has been teaching at Harvest Hill for 14 years and finds it a tremendous challenge. Each child comes to school expecting to be loved and she does her best not to disappoint them. Teaching children like Jayar is helping her to be a better teacher and a better Christian. She tells us,

> The first year that Jayar was in my class I could not reach him. He would cry a lot. He refused to take part in or respond to anything. Toward the end of the year, his mother said she would like me to keep Jayar in my class for one more year, which was a very good idea because he is a slow learner.
>
> In that conversation, his mother told me that even though Jayar would not speak to anyone at school, including me, he would come home and talk about his teacher and how nice she was. That knowledge became my open door to reach Jayar.
>
> Now I praise God for what is happening with this little boy. He still does not smile very often, but he is talking and doing his classwork to the best of his ability. He takes part when we play games in class and seems more at ease.

> *I have learned over the years that through the power of God, a life can be changed. A simple act of God's love can impact a child's life. Jayar is just one of the many little lives that I have seen changed in a positive way at this LACC-sponsored school.*

Mrs. Williams' "job" is her ministry. She asks God for His love and wisdom to do her best every day and feels that the grateful parents like Claudette fuel her strength to excel.

Another person whose life has been changed by Jayar's needs is a social worker who met the boy while serving as a missionary in the area:

> *The day I met Jayar and decided to sponsor him, I was serving as picture taker for the school as they set up case histories on children such as him. It was a very emotional experience — I felt so connected to the children and wanted to help them all.*
>
> *Jayar was repeating the first grade. He consistently hung his head and looked at the floor. His teacher had to coax him to look up for a quick picture. When I realized that he had no sponsor, my choice was made.*
>
> *I've been back to the school several times and although Jayar still doesn't make eye contact with me, he DOES remember my name.*
>
> *I'm honored to be part of Jayar's life and optimistic about his future because of the quality of Christian education he is receiving at Harvest Hill School. It is a pleasure to watch this lad progress from an emotionally damaged child to a healthier student in this good school.*

The prayers, support and devotion of many believers are required to bring about a positive change for a child like Jayar through Latin America ChildCare. And, miraculously, it seems that helping a child through LACC nourishes faith and spiritual growth of all those who help him. How like our Lord to return an extra measure of joy to the giver!

A Hug Heals

As the school director, Coralia, was hosting a tour through the school, a first-grade girl broke away from the others on the playground and — with the biggest smile you have ever seen — came running up to give Coralia a huge hug, then skipped away happily without a word.

Coralia's delight shone almost as brightly as the child's as she explained: Stephany is new to the school. When she had been there only two weeks, Coralia noticed her looking sad and downcast in the hallway. Because she oversees 800 students in the school, Coralia hadn't really gotten to know this one yet, but when she saw the child looking so miserable she felt led to go to her and give her a hug.

The simple gesture of comfort had a disconcerting effect: the little girl began to cry.

Confused, Coralia pulled the child aside and gently encouraged her to talk freely. What emerged was Stephany's story of being passed around from one relative to another all during her six years of life. She never had a secure relationship with a loving adult ... and this was the first hug she could ever remember getting.

Stephany was crying from joy and relief! In that moment, God had used the school director to touch this little child's heart and allowed her to release much anguish.

Since then, Stephany established a new habit: joyously availing herself of Coralia's hugs every day!

Jose's Persistence

From the beginning, Jose's teachers at the Latin America ChildCare-sponsored school knew he was something special. The bright young boy from Panama with the inquisitive eyes loved to learn!

His passion for education had not diminished by the time he graduated from primary school in sixth grade. He kept going!

Then in ninth grade, Jose reached a dilemma. Many students quit school after ninth grade to work for the family. But Jose wanted to keep going to school more than anything. God made a way. He graduated from twelfth grade and gained a scholarship to the University of Panama.

Because of God at work through Latin America ChildCare and sponsors, students like Jose from across Latin America have the opportunity to rise above their situations. And given the opportunity, they will joyously persevere.

Mario

Señor Johnny Esquivel, one of our LACC country directors, had just finished taking two ladies on a tour of a school. Representing a women's group that sponsored two children there, the two had come by to drop off some gifts for the children.

It wasn't a moment that anyone would have expected to be momentous.

Just then one of the teachers came by with a little second grade boy named Mario. The child had a hard and hugely distended stomach due to a serious liver disorder which would shortly take his life, according to the doctors. He was really only in school to make his last days more pleasant.

Johnny and the two ladies immediately agreed to pray for the boy. One woman took a vial of oil from her purse and asked Mario if he believed that Jesus could heal him. The boy said yes, almost without thinking.

After praying over the child, everyone departed and nothing more was said or known ... until one day, the director of the school pointed out a little boy playing ball with the other kids. It was a healthy, whole, fully-healed-by-God ... Mario.

Unfortunately, Mario passed away in 2002 from liver complications. He had several relapses over the past few years, and suffered a lot of pain. He is at peace now with the Lord. His mother, Felicia, who is a cook at the Linda Vista school, is working through the grieving process, but finds joy in the fact that Mario's brother Nilson graduated from 6th grade in December of 2002.

CHAPTER THREE
Changed by Friends
A Tradition of Service

In the schools sponsored by LACC, we tend to think of the children's advancement as a linear progression upward. But if we step back and take a larger view, we see that it is really more like a giant circle, looping back on itself in a tradition of service.

In 1985, Harvest Hill School was founded in Botany Bay, Jamaica, by a woman who accepted no discouragement — Cecile Marie Berg. A missionary from Wisconsin, Cecile answered the need in a community where the children were not going to school.

God impressed on Cecile to begin a school starting with one class, and adding one grade a year until all the children were served. This simple plan encountered lots of problems.

For one, Cecile had to commute from a friend's home in a neighboring community, because she couldn't find a house to rent in the area. Also, she found that her infant school had difficulty maintaining teachers and steady enrollment because of a bad location.

So she continued to canvass the area until she was able to rent a house in that community, and immediately moved the whole school to her house! This improved enrollment and staffing dramatically.

But just when things were getting a little easier, Hurricane Gilbert hit. All the homes in Botany Bay were severely damaged including the school — left with only one roofless room.

In the aftermath of the disaster, without concern for herself, Cecile went into the community to comfort hurt and frightened children. Cecile's neighbor, Vivia McLean, was deeply touched by this example and decided to volunteer her time to cook lunch for the children who came to the school.

Later, when the LACC teams from the U.S. came to build a real schoolhouse, Vivia's enthusiasm spread. Soon her husband and sons were clearing land for the school and helping to put in a road. When a temporary teaching position opened, Cecile asked her long-time volunteer Vivia to become a teacher.

Cecile died in 1993, but her legacy and vision continues in Vivia who is still teaching. Right now she is in charge of two kindergarten classes, with fifty 4- and 5-year-olds!

Vivia's two daughters are graduates from the school: one, Triffeana, is following her mother's footsteps by volunteering in the school. Vivia says:

"I love this school so much"

I love this school so much. The day the founder died was a very sad day for us. My daughter wanted to do cosmetology, but her father died so there was no money to send her to school. She decided to volunteer with me and do like the founder said [because] she always said, 'I am doing it for Jesus!'

Triffeana attended Harvest Hill School from age 4 to 12, then graduated from Seaforth High School when she was 16. At Seaforth, she studied cosmetology and passed her exam, but when her father died, she didn't have the funds to pursue the further schooling needed for a certificate in the field.

In 1999, Triffeana decided to volunteer in the kindergarten class because there were too many students for Vivia to give each one the attention that she wanted to. She gives testimony to God's plan for continuing His schools by establishing a tradition of service:

> *I wanted to give back some of what I had learned from the school. I also wanted to follow in the footsteps of the founder of the school, Cecile Berg. She came here and did all that she could to get this school started and to meet the needs of the community.*

Our newest young teacher is going to continue at the school until she can go back to school herself. In the meantime, teaching has become a new priority to her, and she hopes to teach full-time, doing cosmetology just in her spare time. Triffeana attributes her attitude to Cecile Berg's example and words:

> *I have never stopped believing in the school motto —'Good conduct and hard work are the keys to success.'*

We are so thankful for the godliness of these three women, and for the faithful prayers and support that provide for our students! Lives are being transformed at the LACC-sponsored school and a righteous heritage has been established!

God's Plan — Through 16 Years of Service!

God was at work in Mayra's life, even when she was a little bitty baby.

She was born to an unwed teen with little hope for a successful life. The poor new mother had no baby clothes and fashioned diapers out of old clothes.

When the desperate mother started working at the snack bar of one of our sponsored schools, she brought the baby to work because she did not have a babysitter.

But God had a plan. When little Mayra was old enough, she began kindergarten at the same school.

Now a confident 16-year-old, Mayra is working for her diploma. She is a math tutor, vice president of her student body, attends a devotional at school, and is working on a student campaign about the dangers of AIDS. She is a vibrant member of her local church and hopes to study accounting at the university.

Through God's love and quality education, Latin America ChildCare gives hope to thousands of children like Mayra — hope to rise above the poverty, the rejection, and the hunger that they face daily.

God's Rescue Team

We are grateful and overwhelmed by the way we've seen the Holy Spirit shine in a group of believers at First Assembly of God in Des Moines, Iowa.

When their youth pastor from Des Moines visited our Fuente de Vida school in El Pauji on the outskirts of Caracas, Venezuela, he returned with the seed of an idea for further service, which eventually bore fruit in his congregation.

Taking personally Jesus' command to go into the world and preach the Gospel, a total of 60 Iowans got passports and tickets. The group was divided into two smaller groups: some would provide medical support, and some would build two more floors of classrooms on the current LACC-sponsored school. That second crew would eventually be surprised by God's change of plans.

Clearly, God ordained this trip for a special purpose — not the building of a school, but for flood relief assistance, evangelism, and to bring hope to victims of one of the most catastrophic human tragedies Venezuela has seen.

Upon arrival, the medical crews began their desperately needed clinic duties, and hosted by Pastor Mora of the Fuente de Vida Church, the rest of the Iowans saw firsthand God's new assignment for them as they toured sites that evoked unimaginable horror.

Near El Pauji, a mountainside community called La Quebrada now only exists in the memories of the survivors ... since three mid-December days brought 35 inches of rain. Torrents of mud and boulders killed countless thousands as the wall of mud, water and rock cut five paths — each from 75 to 150 feet wide — down the ravines from the mountains to the Caribbean coast.

Upon viewing the devastation, one worker said she had come to understand "why God called 60 people down here."

The Iowans climbed through former neighborhoods, reduced to dried mud and debris, with iron beams twisted like spaghetti and vehicles mangled beyond recognition. Death toll estimates ranged wildly from 30,000 to 150,000 — everyone lost family or friends.

Not surprisingly, Venezuela was ill-prepared to care for more than 100,000 refugees. Months later, living in shelters and makeshift homes along the edge of the wall of mud, survivors must still rely on relief agencies for food. Everyone agrees that relocating these folks will take years.

Hiking through the disaster zone, the new missionaries were further sobered by testimonies of locals and sights like ... a tiny tennis shoe emerging from the floor of mud.

More than 100 Venezuelans committed their lives to Christ

Jose Roure pointed out a place of boulders and mud hardened like concrete that used to be his home, a site he hopes is his mother's grave. There is no way to be sure — many bodies were washed out to sea. Pointing to a nearby cross, and potted flowers, he prefers to think of her resting there in her home.

Ramon speaks no English, but tells all with a gesture and a word — "cadaver"— <u>corpse</u>. Unknown thousands are buried in the Quebrada Seca, which eerily means, "Dry Ravine."

Rosa Aguirre gives glory and praise to God for sparing the lives of her family. The morning of December 17, unsettled by the amount of rain falling, she took her three children with her when she left to clean houses — and their home was swept away behind them!

As the community restoration began, nationals and missionaries working together were all amazed by one local volunteer. Neco or "Cripple" as he was known, was born with tiny deformed legs. But he made a solid contribution and inspired awe in everyone by sitting on the ground, enthusiastically digging dirt and mixing cement. Neco's niece is a student at the school and he was proud to be a part of the relief effort.

And as the Iowans worked and ministered, every person they treated for illness or injury brought their children to see the puppet shows put on by the missionaries, and was asked the question: "Do you have Jesus in your heart?"

Through interpreters and booklets written in Spanish, they told people about Jesus. More than 100 Venezuelans committed their lives to Jesus during that visit, in clinics, work sites, and in emotional altar calls that followed the puppet shows.

Pastor Palmer preached in the rain one evening, with Mary Mahon, missionary to the school, to interpret, declaring "Satan has come to kill and destroy, but Jesus has come to give life ... It is more than just believing in your head, it's trusting in your heart!" Then a familiar tune — with Spanish words — was lifted up, and the strains of "Cuan Grande Es El" ("How Great Thou Art") rose to the clouds that hovered in the mountain ridges above the worshippers!

While the yet-unfinished school in El Pauji serves the needs of uprooted children in the area, the staff is primarily using the facilities to reach out to refugees, and performing almost more as a community center than school during this crisis.

As for the school building, steel reinforcement rods still point skyward from the roof as a silent reminder of the objective that was completely ignored. As the Iowans met together one last time before departure, volunteer Steve Drake pointed to the awkward spires and vowed, "We will come back and help you complete it."

We know that all supporters do not swing picks or hammers, but we all build, staff, and enable these LACC-sponsored schools, through the impact of our prayers and faithful giving.

And yes, the school is still unimproved, but as the volunteers from Des Moines discovered when they purposed to build a school, and instead helped to restore a whole community: with God you can completely miss your goal, and still achieve the desires of your heart!

Gang Member Transformed

If Alexander Javier isn't the biggest seventh-grader at Nueva Vida school in Nicaragua, then he's definitely the oldest ... at 19!

Alexander got a late start in school, because he had spent much of his earlier years hanging out with his fellow gang members. Regularly, the gang would come around the school to harass the students.

Then the school's teachers began visiting his house once a week, encouraging Alexander to attend church. Eventually, he started showing up at the church services ... and he gave his life to Christ! His gang members soon followed him.

Saved and separated from his life as a gang member, Alexander wanted to learn. Then 18, he was too old to start school since he had dropped out in fourth or fifth grade, but the school made an exception and placed him in the sixth grade. Alexander, now in seventh-grade, is adored by his fellow students and teachers.

Alexander is also a deacon in his church and has been given the responsibilities of the keys to the church. In addition to preaching, Alexander is in charge of an outreach ministry at his school and a ministry at his church, to which he often brings his friends.

> *Saved and separated from his life as a gang member, Alexander wanted to learn*

This young man may be doing things unconventionally, but God is using him to make a tremendous impact in his school and community!

A Series of Good Decisions

Decades ago, Harvey Kaufman made a decision to follow Christ. Years later, in 1994, he decided to share the love of God that had changed his life — through Latin America ChildCare. This Arizona resident now sponsors three children through LACC.

Then, just two years ago, Harvey noticed a flyer about gift annuities that arrived with his monthly receipt letter. Intrigued, Harvey returned the coupon to ask for more information.

After speaking with the LACC representative, Harvey decided to set up a gift annuity to benefit LACC. He has also named Latin America ChildCare as the sole beneficiary of his estate.

Why?

"I wanted to bless the Lord's work, and also wanted to help children living in poor conditions get a good start in life," Harvey said. "I wanted to help these children for the Lord while they are young and in their formative years."

Thanks to Harvey's decisions over the past several years, children in Latin America and the Caribbean will be blessed by his love and compassion for years to come!

A Calling Becomes a Family Tradition of Missions

Bueno. It means "good" in Spanish.

But to Latin America ChildCare, Bueno is more than good. It is the last name of our founder and his wife, John and Lois Bueno, who more than 40 years ago became visionaries, friends and mentors to thousands, and missionary heroes at LACC.

John's life included varied job descriptions, from life as a missionary kid in Chile, to becoming the Executive Director of

Assemblies of God World Missions. And considering the level of esteem in which he is held at LACC, it's gratifying to know that it is his wife, Lois, who is his quiet hero.

Lois was just 20 years old, and a newlywed when she went to El Salvador. And she didn't speak a word of Spanish! But she learned the language from talking to her friends every day, and kept very busy raising four very active boys — three of whom are now missionaries in El Salvador.

Beginning her own ministry for women called Koinonia, Lois' vision neatly dovetailed into the larger picture. Koinonia was involved in dozens of activities, not the least of which was providing hundreds of scholarships for the most needy children in the Latin America ChildCare schools.

Lois is a great mother, and a wonderful example as well. Now John and Lois' son Bob and his wife Cilinia are missionaries working with Latin America ChildCare, and they also present a Christian television program called "Algo Bueno," which is more than a play on their last name, in Spanish it means "Something Good."

Algo Bueno in Spanish means "Something Good"

John and Lois' sons David and Ron, along with Ron's wife, Michelle, and David's wife, Heather, work with the community development ministry called ENLACE. ENLACE assists communities where LACC-sponsored schools are located with special medical care, clean water projects and even with vocational training and small microenterprise businesses.

The first school that the Buenos founded in El Salvador is still ministering to children daily, and that school has served as a prototype for over 300 schools we have throughout Latin America. And as John continued the tradition of Christian service from his parents, so have their children taken direction from them.

The Buenos were called of God to begin, and build up, a marvelous service for Him. They are more than "Bueno" to us!

Ruth Sandoval:
Specially-Selected Messenger

A phone call in the middle of the night always makes your heart and mind race. Such a call is seldom news you are looking forward to. Such was the case when the word came that Ruth Sandoval had died.

Ruth was one of the original teachers in the first Latin America ChildCare school we ever attempted in Costa Rica. She faithfully served as teacher in our program for almost 15 years, then suddenly, unexpectedly, died of a heart attack at the age of 35.

Ruth is with the Lord now, and we hope she has had many wonderful conversations with Him about her ministry at Latin America ChildCare — her life's avocation. I have no doubt that He is delighted with all her efforts to nurture and educate His precious children here. We rejoice with her in the change that has brought her directly into the presence of our Lord, even while we deal with the loss of her in our lives.

Her funeral was a beautiful event to behold.

Several hundred of her former students, dressed in their school uniforms, attended her funeral. Their lives serve as living witness to Ruth's contribution toward the Kingdom of God! Many of them took the opportunity to publicly testify to the difference that Ruth had made in their lives. And this was so appropriate, because her entire adult life had been dedicated to serving Jesus Christ through Latin America ChildCare.

For two shifts a day, year in and year out, Ruth had given her life in service to the children of Latin America ... some of whom would have had no chance at survival without her prayerful efforts. She was God's specially-selected messenger for these children. Every time she invested love, or compassion, or the good news of Jesus Christ into their lives, I know it touched the heart of our Heavenly Father.

Ruth was one of hundreds of teachers, in 300 schools, serving 80,000 children every day. She was part of a miracle we call Latin

America ChildCare, within a larger miracle called Salvation Through Jesus Christ. And now she is resting from her work, and her students show every promise of following in the example that she left for them.

CHAPTER FOUR
Changed by Christ
Quality, Professionalism... and the Glory of God!

In an open letter to Latin America ChildCare, George Stamos' first statement was a real attention grabber:

> *My family is doubling our financial support of Latin America ChildCare after a recent visit to the LACC schools in Nicaragua.*

George and his wife were part of a team of 16 educators who took a staff development seminar to our teachers in Nicaragua.

> *We had many memorable experiences and impressions, but the most vivid impression of this whole experience is the quality of the schools we visited, the professionalism of the teachers we worked with, and the glory of God revealed through the pastors and missionaries in Central America.*

George was glowing in his praise for our teachers in four different staff development sessions, asserting that his school would welcome a team of LACC teachers to instruct them in teaching methodologies. He found that our teachers were amazing!

> *Teachers learn to live with intrusions, but our intrusion in the classroom ... was exceptional. Sixteen teachers walking through a small school is very noticeable ... Add to that, teachers who are taking pictures, conversing in a foreign language, and talking to students in their own language, and the potential for absolute chaos is very apparent. However these teachers continued to guide students through their exercises, the students continued to learn and they were on their best behavior. It was a real tribute to the professional attitudes of the teachers.*

> *He found out that our teachers were amazing*

Mr. Stamos spoke of the excellent caliber of students that he encountered at our schools in Nicaragua, finding them to be indicators of the level of the commitment to learning in the teachers and pastors involved in the schools.

The commitment to excellence was also evidenced in that some of the seminar participants had to travel twelve hours in extreme heat to attend these classes, and they definitely came to interact and to learn. The American team found the local teachers to be very strong indeed. In one case, the participants expanded the lesson to show other ways that the assignment in question could be made more meaningful to the students. Mr. Stamos says,

> *One of our goals was to encourage these teachers to begin a system of staff development seminars taught by their own teachers. We came away with the knowledge that these teachers, pastors, and missionaries are very capable of organizing, directing, and teaching these seminars throughout Nicaragua and Central America!*

Latin America ChildCare ~ Providing Hope

SOME OF OUR HISTORY

John & Lois Bueno in May of 1962, after first arriving in El Salvador.

8th grade girls standing on the roof of their school, wearing the school's first uniforms in 1964.

1983 ~ Fourth grade class at school 0115

1983 ~ Children receiving their food at school 0102

1989 ~ Christmas gift distribution to children at school 0102

Members of the board/elders of Church (Templo Cristiano), praying for the Bueno's at their retirement service (from El Salvador)

Latin America ChildCare
Providing Hope

A PHOTO ESSAY

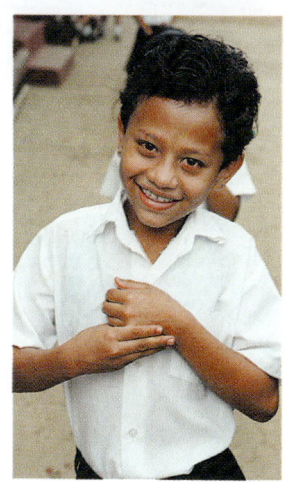

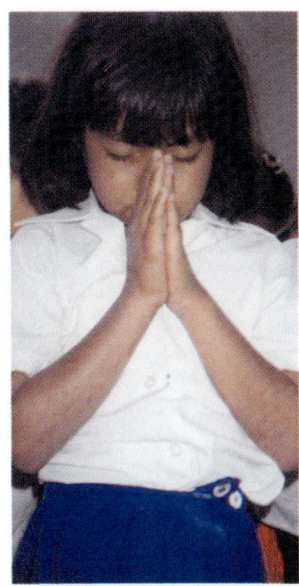

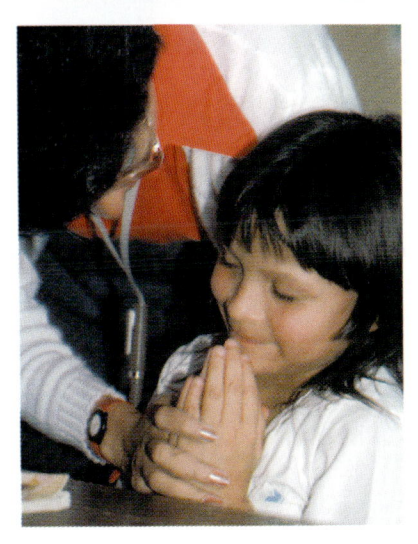

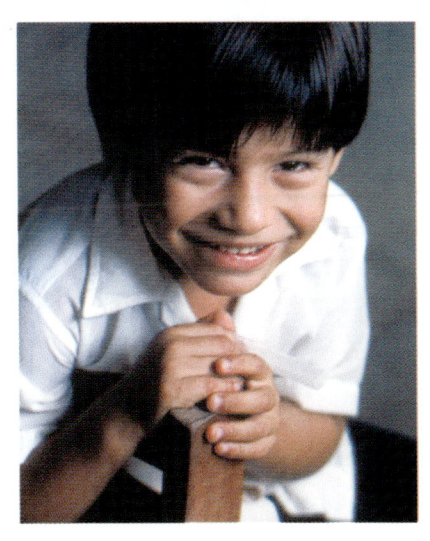

Providing Hope ~ Latin America ChildCare Life Stories

Providing Hope ~ Latin America ChildCare Life Stories

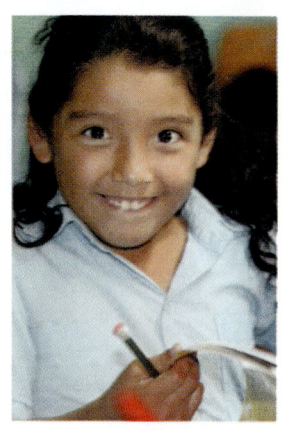

Providing Hope ~ Latin America ChildCare Life Stories

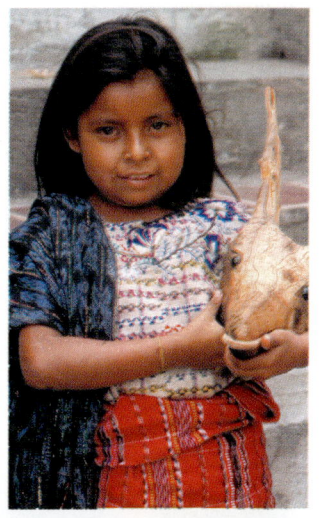

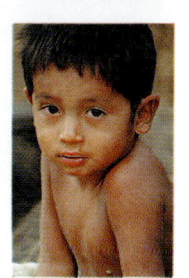

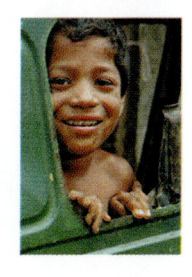

Providing Hope ~ Latin America ChildCare Life Stories

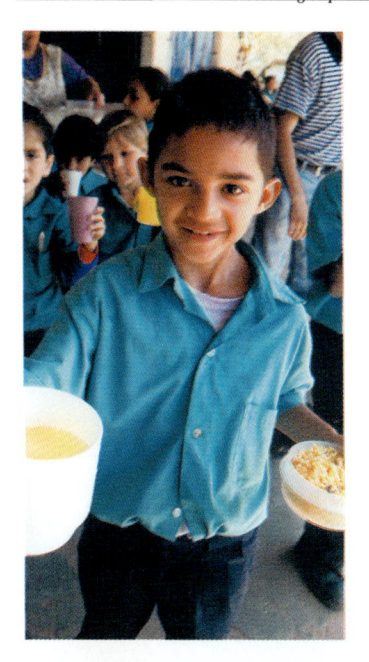

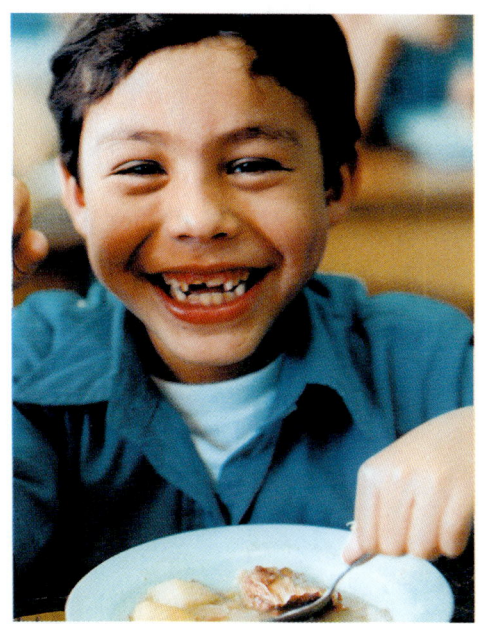

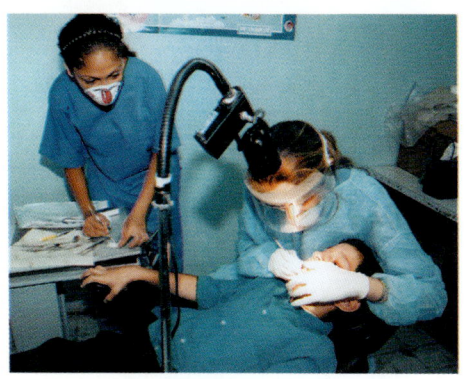

Providing Hope ~ Latin America ChildCare Life Stories

Providing Hope ~ Latin America ChildCare Life Stories

The most memorable part of the trip for Mr. and Mrs. Stamos was seeing the glory of God being revealed through the students, teachers and pastors. He acknowledges being very impressed by every person he met at the LACC-sponsored schools in Nicaragua:

> My family has been a sponsor of LACC for a number of years. We are interested in education by vocation, and LACC seemed like a natural place for us to support.
>
> Generally, when we give, we give 'as unto the Lord.' After this experience in Nicaragua, I know that the money sent is used in a mighty way.
>
> Our family is doubling our sponsorship of LACC because we know that it is money well spent! We saw it through the eyes of the students, the determination of the teachers, and the vision of the pastors and missionaries.
>
> I think everyone should double their support. It is an investment in eternity.

Thanks George. We couldn't have said it better ourselves!

Wendy

Wendy lives in El Salvador. She is six. She lives with her father who is blind and cannot protect her. In an amazingly short conversation, the tragedy of her life circumstance was illuminated:

> "Where do you live, Wendy?"
>
> "I live with my daddy."
>
> "Where is your mother?"
>
> "I don't know."

"What do you want to do when you grow up?"

"I want to sell cigarettes and lottery tickets like my daddy."

Doesn't it make you want to pull this little child up on your lap and soothe her worries away?

Part of our vision at Latin America ChildCare — what we offer to Wendy and children like her throughout Latin America and the Caribbean — is "the lap of God." This ministry is a place where God can pull these little ones away from danger and worry.

While sponsors, teachers, and staff take care of the physical, mental and emotional needs ... Jesus is protecting them, soothing them and showing them a safe path for their lives. Just as a parent might rock a child in his arms.

Juan and Carlos

Juan and Carlos of Peru know about terrorism first-hand — they've seen the violence and they live with its devastation. When these brothers were but young teens, they witnessed a horror no one should be forced to endure, especially children.

Juan and Carlos saw their parents being murdered. They helplessly watched as members of Shining Path — a group of guerilla government fighters — snuffed out the lives of their mom and dad. Their world would never be the same.

Orphaned with nowhere to go, and no one to care for them, the brothers found a home in the back of a busy bakery. To avoid living on the streets, they awoke at 3 a.m. every morning — day after day after day — to bake bread.

They then sold the bread and were allowed to eat some. Bread became their livelihood ... their means of survival. In fact, bread was the only food they had to eat.

Just when life seemed hopeless for these malnourished orphans, they found the compassion of Christ through a local Latin America ChildCare-sponsored school. The two were determined to gain an education. They kept up their work in the bakery and were allowed to attend school after baking and selling bread.

When the brothers first attended school, no one thought they would be able to accomplish much — they were malnourished, lonely boys. But God had a plan. Through the school feeding program, the boys began eating a nutritional meal, and their grades shot up.

The school purchased computers, and the boys began moving to the head of their class in this area of study and others. Now, Juan has the opportunity to study computer programming at a university. God helped Juan and Carlos triumph over tragedy.

Kenneth

So many students come to our Latin America ChildCare program from tragic circumstances. As much as it hurts us to see and motivates us to help, it isn't an unusual occurrence.

Each of us prays to stay soft to the children and their needs from the first day, so we can really reach out and minister, and pray effectively for each child. And God often brings us a little person with a story so sad, our hearts are crushed. Like Kenneth.

He is a seven-year-old attending one of our schools in Costa Rica. Before he came to our school, he suffered more misery than a child should ever have to cope with on his own.

Last year, the little boy's mother committed suicide ... hanging herself ... and killing her unborn child in the process.

Kenneth was passed along to his grandmother for a while, and then passed again to an aunt.

To top it all off, at his previous school, the children taunted and teased him cruelly about these events for which he was not to blame, and over which he had no control. The little guy spent every day feeling miserable and lost.

But his aunt had compassion for him, and a few months ago he was transferred to one of the schools supported by Latin America ChildCare.

And what a transformation! Kenneth loves it there, especially the stories about Jesus — and he's never had so much loving attention as he has from his teacher. As for his classmates — not only do they not tease him — he's made new friends!

Kenneth still has his struggles. He's not an A-student. Although he's repeating the 4th grade, he has not given up and says he wants to do better this year. His home situation is still unstable, but he is getting all the love and reassurance he needs to rebuild his young life from his teachers and the principal, Coralia Bonilla. And he is learning to lean on Jesus for all his needs.

Karen

Karen Garcia's world fell apart before she hardly had time to live much of it. Her mother died and she did not know her father — the young girl felt completely and utterly alone. Her father traveled to Brazil to meet her for the first time and asked her to live with him in Bolivia. Karen was frightened, but agreed. She began attending Luz y Verdad School, sponsored by Latin America ChildCare.

> *Karen remembers the moment that changed her life*

Her teacher, Rosalia Rodriguez Navia, saw an angry, hurting little girl. "Karen was a proud girl ... a girl that had many problems for different reasons." Karen laughed and made fun of God — at first.

Karen remembers the moment that changed her life: "One day I asked my teacher why all of the students talked so much about God and His wonderful works? Why didn't I know Him? Then my teacher invited me to accept Jesus as my Savior. She read her Bible to me and I felt a wonderful experience. The Lord changed my life."

Her teacher said Karen "understood she was living an empty life.

She opened her heart to Jesus Christ and He changed her life. Now she is different."

A week later Karen received a letter from her sponsor, Linda Walters of Milwaukee, Wisconsin.

"I felt proud and happy because she wrote me," Karen said. "To have a sponsor is like having a sister because you have the opportunity to share many things. My school Luz y Verdad is like my second home because students and teachers are a big family, a family joined in Jesus Christ."

Linda said Karen "is a wonderful girl — the recent letters show me how much she has grown. I am happy to be her sponsor."

A Prayer for a Sponsor

Sometimes just a few words can change your whole life.

For Alicia, those words came from the director of her school: "You have a sponsor!"

The little girl was so excited. She immediately sat down to write a lady named Dorothy in the United States, who had cared enough to give her the security of a sponsorship for her Christian education:

> *Dear Sponsor Dorothy,*
>
> *I am so happy to hear that you have decided to help me. I have been praying for a sponsor for a long time.*
>
> *I am 10 years old ... and I do not have a mom or a dad. I live with my grandma and grandpa. They told me that my mom died when I was born. I do not know who my father is.*

My grandparents are so nice to me and I love them very much. My grandma is 69 years old and my grandpa is 80 years old. My grandpa grows corn and my grandma takes care of the house. I help her clean, run errands, and wash our clothes in the river.

I am so happy to be attending this Christian school. My teacher tells us Bible stories and every day I try to be a good student. Last year, I was the best student.

I walk an hour every day to school and I have to cross two rivers. Right now, it is winter and it rains a lot.

I am sending you a picture. Please send me a picture so I can see what you look like.

With much love,
Alicia

More than just a letter of sincere thanks, this child responded in love and trust to a stranger who had already reached out to her. It is the beginning of a relationship grounded in the selfless love of Christ and the compassionate generosity of one of His children to another.

It is always our prayer that the dependable generosity of a sponsor will not only be an investment in the life of a child ... but just maybe ... the friendship of a lifetime!

Matching Sacrifices

To say that all of the children who receive a solid education and daily nourishment at our schools are appreciative would be an understatement. Almost all of the children that we serve through LACC have known deprivation of some sort. And we think this is part of why so many of them excel beyond any expectation.

But once in a while, one student stands out, not just because of academic excellence, but also by their obvious dedication to their schooling. In the face of pressures that would be understandable — reasons to just give up, get a job and forget education — young Juanito has never let his schooling lag.

He lives so far away from the closest school in El Salvador, his home is almost in Guatemala. He must get up early to complete his chores at home, then ride three hours on a bus, one-way, just to get to the school. And this is no comfortable, air-conditioned bus ride either. It is just what you might visualize — a hot, dusty Salvadorian countryside bus.

Classes run all afternoon, then he faces a long trip home on the crowded, squeaky bus. It is often after eight in the evening when his parents see him again. Still he is up early and back on the bus to get to school.

Now you might think that no one could expect more from a youngster — that his plate was more than full — but that isn't the reality of poor Salvadorian life.

Many poor families simply cannot afford to have their older children tied up in school every day — when they are needed to help subsidize the family. In order to be able to attend school — an investment of virtually all daylight — and some after dark hours — Juanito had to come up with a plan to help his family financially.

So Juanito has a small business. He sells juice and snacks to other bus riders on his trip to and from school, to make his time profitable for the family.

So this lad is faithful to his family by providing funds for them — and faithful to his education, riding the bus for six hours a day to attend — and faithful to God as a promising young Christian.

Juanito exemplifies the gratefulness of the LACC students as a whole, and yet, he has a greater spark. His ambition and good attitude, coupled with God's blessing, could open many doors for him.

Juanito has matched the faithfulness and sacrifice of his sponsor with faithfulness and sacrifice of his own.

This is one indication that the ministry of LACC is helping to change the face of Latin America for Christ. We have reason to expect that Juanito will become a fine man, making godly decisions, and serving to lead his community in those right paths too.

A Neighborhood Helps Its Own

We are fond of pointing out, from time to time, that it takes four people to make Latin America ChildCare happen: a child, a sponsor, a teacher and the Savior.

And it is true that God calls at least three into alliance to allow a child to grow emotionally, spiritually and physically in our program. But, usually, we tend to think of at least one, if not two of those parts will come from outside of Latin America. That's frequently true but ...

... it's entirely possible for everyone involved to have originated in Latin America or the Caribbean.

A good example is the three that God called together when Irma Bermalina Cortez sponsored Marcela Beatriz Rodriguez.

Latin America ChildCare sponsorship programs exist throughout the hemisphere. In El Salvador, the sponsorship program is called "Piedad," and one of Piedad's most enthusiastic sponsors is Irma, who views this as a way of reflecting her own experience of "God's love for me."

"I want to love and help the children"

"I want to love and help the children," she says. "There are so many people who are in need in our country, but the children need the help the most. Only Christ can transform them from the inside. We need to reach these children with the Gospel, and they can be witnesses to their parents."

Marcella is a seventh grader in the Campestre School. Marcela has been attending Campestre for four years, and she always says she is very grateful for Irma's help.

"I really enjoy going to this school, and have made many close friends here," the student testifies. "I am now involved after school in the Castle Club evangelism team. We share the gospel through drama and song to children in different neighborhoods."

The third element of this "team" is Yanira Ponce De Sandoval, who has been observing the youngster's intellectual and spiritual growth firsthand over the last three years. She really likes what she sees, and knows that a big part of why that growth has been possible is Irma's sponsorship.

"It is wonderful that Marcela's sponsor has made it possible for her to attend this school," Yanira says. Yanira, like all of the teachers at Campestre School is a big believer in what the program is doing for individual students, and the communities that they serve as well.

The Latin America ChildCare program draws four parts together, and it works no matter where any of them come from. In this case, Marcella's help — Irma and Yanira — came from her own backyard!

A School Lunch Saves a Life?

When Justin began to attend an LACC-sponsored school, he was obviously malnourished. This is not uncommon, and usually we are gratified to see the quality lunches that the school supplies begin to fill out the little frames right away. But in Justin's case, that didn't happen.

The longer he attended, the thinner he got. It was baffling.

Every day the staff was providing for Justin and the others. We watched as Justin enjoyed every morsel on his plate, but he just wasn't getting any stronger.

Finally, the school director decided to make a visit to the child's home, a one room bamboo shack with parents and four little sisters and brothers ... and in the process made a shocking discovery!

Because the rising inflation had hit his family so hard, there simply wasn't enough food to feed all the children in the family, so his mother had been forced to make the decision to feed only the youngest children.

Not only that, but Justin was getting up early every morning to help his parents and engaging in intensive manual labor, before attending school in the afternoon.

The only meal the boy had was what we gave him at lunch, and that just wasn't enough nourishment for the rigorous workload placed upon him.

But he never once complained, never mentioned it to anyone. He was just so happy to be able to come to school, to learn lessons, know Jesus — and receive his one-and-only meal of the day!

Armed with this new knowledge, the director was able to arrange with the staff for extra portions of milk and oatmeal to be supplied. Now, after five months, a filled-out Justin is the picture of health!

Unfortunately, with skyrocketing inflation throughout Latin America, this story could be about any child. Stories like this are becoming more and more common, with mothers having to decide which of their children will eat and which will go hungry.

The extreme value of Latin America ChildCare — in the lives of needy children in impoverished countries — is ratified day after day.

When a child gains a sponsor, a quality education is assured ... a child is introduced to Christ, and has the chance to love and serve Him ... and most children can count on at least one solid meal a day.

Perhaps one day, the needs of the children in Latin America and the Caribbean will be so abundantly supplied that sponsors won't be needed there any more — that would be wonderful. But until that time, we'll pray for more sponsors, for little guys like Justin.

Changed Forever

In Ayacucho, Peru, young Lizbeth Evangelina Mendoza did not have an easy life. Although fortunate enough to have Latin America ChildCare sponsors who loved her, she was almost forced to drop out of school entirely.

Her father had abandoned her and her mom to fend for themselves, and the only way they could survive was through selling homemade bread on the corner. The pressure of providing for the family on her own was too much for Mom — she ended up in the hospital. Then Dad reappeared in Lizbeth's life: he had been hospitalized with a back injury, and now he wanted his family's help.

It was all too much for one little girl! She couldn't take care of her parents and go to school. Even when Mom got back on her feet, Lizbeth continued to stay by her side and help her sell the tasty "chaplas" bread they made.

But Lizbeth's sponsors, the Sheridan family of Ft. Collins, had not forgotten about her. When they heard that Phyllis Kovac would visit her daughter Gwen Kovac, a missionary in Peru, they asked her to take a gift to Lizbeth.

Lizbeth was thrilled to receive the present! And Gwen and Phyllis had the opportunity to talk to her mother about making sure Lizbeth went back to school. When Mom arrived at school the next day to get Lizbeth back in class, the Kovacs spoke with her about Jesus and led her to the Lord!

Our Country Coordinator for Peru, Christina Frigoli, stopped by to purchase some "chaplas" bread the other day, and she said the change in Lizbeth's Mom is remarkable. She says it is hard to believe this is the same beaten-down and broken woman who came to re-enroll Lizbeth in school — instead she has joy in her eyes and a wonderful smile on her face!

One Last Chance at Hope

Evelyn Peña Diwelin was at the point of committing suicide. She didn't know she had any other options.

The 45-year-old single mother of five was battling uterine and throat cancer. Without insurance or financial assistance to help with the high medical costs, she was forced to spend much of the family's meager income on her medication and treatment ... and that meant the children often went without food.

Evelyn was desperate for something to change. She thought her only escape was taking her own life.

But she decided to try one last thing — and she composed a note to the director of the LACC-sponsored school in Costa Rica where her three youngest children attend, asking for help.

About that same time, the school's teachers and director had noticed that Evelyn's fifth-grade daughter was missing school regularly. When they asked her why, she explained her family's tragic situation.

Then Evelyn's note arrived. The school director immediately went into action to help the family.

Thankfully, she had an excellent resource — the "Extreme Poverty Fund" supported by the friends and sponsors of LACC. This fund allowed the school to provide the struggling family with food for three months — shoes, clothing, notebooks, and other necessities — as well as periodic assistance with food further down the road.

Evelyn is extremely grateful. The school and their willingness to help her and her children is what saved her life, she said. The school's love and compassion brought hope to her family!

God Takes First Place

In the slums of Guayaquil, Ecuador, Martha Susetty Gonzalez Pavsn was given very little ... but she took it ... and ran ... literally!

A Latin America ChildCare student, Martha has taken first place in Ecuador's national track meet and has placed in international meets as well.

An excellent student as well, she has now been awarded a scholarship to continue her training at the Cordovez Carlin Center in Havana, Cuba.

Like most of the 4,700 students of Liceo Christiano de Guayaquil, Martha is from a very poor home. Her father deserted the family of five children. But now the youngsters have found what their mother calls a "second home" at our school.

"I think that without this school, I wouldn't be able to know that God loves me," Martha says. "I thank the Lord for giving me this opportunity, and for all my teachers. All my achievements will be for Jesus Christ, and for His glory."

When Martha first took part in the athletics program at our Guayaquil school, it was the first time it was ever offered. She is now in 11th grade and specializes in courses in computer technology.

> *"Without this school, I wouldn't be able to know that God loves me"*

Martha is a prime example of why LACC is planning to put computer centers into the schools, starting with the larger secondary schools. Like everywhere else in the world, globalization has provided job markets for graduates that are equipped to accept them. Soon Martha will be the first of many graduates of Liceo Christiano de Guayaquil that will make their living in the computer field.

"I am proud of being a student at Liceo," Martha says. "I like to keep the name of the Lord first place in each of my acts."

For Martha, training in Cuba will mean the opportunity to participate in more international competitions and larger track meets. So remember her name and be watching for Martha as she runs for her future — with Jesus in her heart!

A Sponsor's Love
by John and Mary Anthony

"… and on some have compassion, making a difference."
(Jude 2:2 KJV)

When my wife, Mary, and I filled out our application to sponsor two children, one boy and one girl, we had no idea that we would soon be visiting their Latin American location as LACC volunteers.

We were delighted to be assigned to the LACC-sponsored school in Villa Riva, Dominican Republic. This is an historic community whose 10,000 residents live among rice and sugar cane fields in much the same way as their ancestors have for 400 years.

On the day of our arrival, we met Anabel, the fourth grade girl that we sponsor. Throughout the next three weeks she and my wife Mary spent hours together, forming a precious relationship.

Anabel is intelligent and talented, although very shy. She has lived in the care of her maternal grandmother since she was three months old. She loves Sunday school and playing the tambourine.

Mary taught Anabel her English lessons and how to cross-stitch. Anabel taught Mary to play the favorite Dominican game of dominos, and spoke patiently and slowly in Spanish so that her new "patrocinadora" understood everything.

Anabel was thrilled, because God had shown her that He knows where she lives — by bringing her sponsors to her! It also began to sink in that she was now a newly sponsored student at the school, not just attending until a sponsor could be found.

After connecting with this dear little girl, we turned our attention to finding the nine-year-old boy we sponsored, Rubén. We found out that his paperwork hadn't cleared yet. But three days later his mother brought a beaming boy to us. Rubén had just learned of his new sponsorship and was so excited to meet us that his shyness was short-lived. We shook hands and he realized that his life was really going to change after the school break when he would start attending this Christian school.

Our last day of work was also the last day of school — the "Día de los Niños" — where all the children assembled in chapel to receive a gift from their sponsors. The school staff also prepared a wonderful feast of barbecued chicken and rice and beans for all the students and visitors.

Anabel and Rubén wouldn't normally have been included in all these festivities because they were so newly sponsored, but the Lord made a special provision.

We gave Anabel her much-prayed-for dolls, and Rubén his longed-for tow truck. Mary and I were delighted to see them run around to show their still-wrapped gifts to the other children. They felt loved and included.

Because he lived so far away, we drove Rubén home. His face beamed as he rode in our big truck and gave directions to his "casa." We turned off the main road onto a dirt path lined with banana and palm trees, then around a corner until he called for us to stop.

His mother greeted us, new baby in arms, and invited us inside the wood-sided, tin-roofed house. Soon we were sitting in two of the three chairs in their sparsely furnished living rooms. The wall was decorated with two big calendar pictures and the floor was concrete, something unusual for such a poor family. Two naked light bulbs lit the joyful scene as Rubén finally opened his wrapped gift in front of his stepfather, two sisters and many neighborhood children who had gathered for this unique event.

I suggested that we take a family photo outside, and then we hugged and shook hands before we drove off. When we return to work in the area again in February, we will bring a first-ever family photo to Rubén's parents.

But even more wonderful, we had the joy of seeing a new beginning in Rubén's life, and soon his family will be exposed to the life-changing power of the Gospel through this humble LACC school's ministry. A solid Christian education is the only hope of breaking through the bondage of poverty and slaying the death grip of ignorance upon this young boy's life.

As a post-script, I would add that we have been informed that Rubén was used to being laughed at because he is small for his age, making him shy. But since his teacher, Tier Daliga, told his class the story of Zaccheus and also about Emperor Napoleon, Rubén has not felt inferior because of his small stature. He says that we are all big in God's eyes!

Johnny

Missionary Mary Mahon came to El Paují, Venezuela to help launch a Christian school, and she attended Fuente de Vida Church, which would work in tandem with the school.

Each time she arrived in El Paují for work or church, a four-year-old boy named Johnny would show up and cling to her. He was dirty and unkempt, and Mary wondered where his parents or brothers and sisters were — and why no one seemed to look out for Johnny.

Says Mary, "Oftentimes I shared my lunch with him. Other times he would go to sleep on my lap in service or sometimes in my car. I believe he found a refuge in the church and later in the school."

Johnny did have parents nearby, but Ali and Yelitza did not have much time for their children. They were both in bondage to drugs and alcohol. Johnny had brothers, too: an older brother named Gilbert, and a younger brother named Angelito.

Gilbert was actually supposed to attend the closest public school to their home, but he had been threatened by violent gangs so many times on his way to school, he had just quit going.

When the Christian school Mary was helping to launch was finally up and running, Johnny and Gilbert were both enrolled. That's when Mary finally discovered who Johnny's parents were.

Yelitza came to the school to ask for prayer.

She knew that her children were suffering because she could not be a good mother to them, and she knew that drugs and alcohol were destroying her and her family. Joel, one of the teachers, began to share with Yelitza about the love of Jesus.

Yelitza made a confession of faith and contacted the pastor of Fuente de Vida church. The congregation made an effort to reach out to Yelitza, and slowly her life began to change. Within a year, she had defeated her drug and alcohol addiction!

"I am thankful to God for being the drug rehab center in my life," Yelitza says.

Yelitza even began a cell group Bible study in her home. Ali, the father of her children, came home to hear the singing of the Christians, and something about what he heard touched his heart. Soon he, too, had given his life to Christ!

The Lord freed him from drug and alcohol addiction, and he says he feels stronger physically and spiritually now — and he loves waking up without a hangover on Monday mornings!

Ali is committed to church and is a regular at the all-night prayer meetings.

Mary says, "Yelitza is very strong in the Lord. She and several people in her cell group have made a commitment to visit the sick in homes and hospitals and preach the word and teach them the Bible. Yelitza has a burden for the women she used to use drugs with. She prays for them and uses every opportunity to share the Lord with them."

Sister Dora, one of the Fuente de Vida Board Members says of Yelitza, "She is

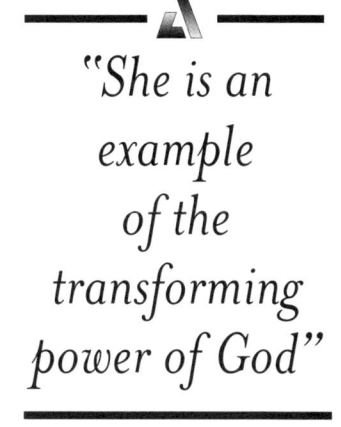

> "She is an example of the transforming power of God"

an example of the Transforming Power of God."

The people of the community are stunned by this total transformation of Yelitza, Ali and their sons, because they have known the couple for years. One neighbor called the change in Yelitza "a miracle," and he was so inspired by it, he came to church to discover the power that had transformed her. He committed his life to the Lord, too!

Today, all three of Yelitza's sons are enrolled in school. Gilbert, who had fallen behind in his studies because he was afraid of the gangs at his old school, has rapidly caught up with his grade. Mary says Johnny has learned to read and write and sometimes reads the Bible aloud to her.

And the youngest boy, Angelito, loves school and church, and says he wants to be a pastor when he grows up.

Yelitza and Ali have a new baby girl, and they are praying that their four teenage girls will soon come to know Jesus, too. Please pray with them for this important need.

Stories like the transformation of Yelitza and Ali — and their sons — aren't uncommon in communities throughout Latin America wherever faithful friends have put Latin America ChildCare ministry into action. We are so grateful that through the beautiful commitment of our partners and child sponsors, stories like this are possible!

A Really BIG Family

In the beginning, they didn't envision themselves as sponsors to 16 children ... but one sponsored child led to another ... and another ... and another ...

... and each child was so unique and so fascinating that they couldn't bear the thought of being without any one of them in their extended Latin American family of sponsored children.

Originally, Mr. and Mrs. Murphree became interested in becoming Latin America ChildCare sponsors after they read an ad in the

EVANGEL. They contacted our office and asked if they could sponsor a little boy in the country of Paraguay — though they didn't know anything about the Latin American country or its poor economic state.

Soon, little Candido's picture came in the mail. Then came letters from the child, expressing his love and appreciation for their sponsorship. Over time, Mr. and Mrs. Murphree began to learn about Candido's school and his church ... and they fell in love with the little boy.

In time, the Murphrees sponsored another child, and then another, and another. Their compassionate ministry for Christ began to branch out into other parts of the world — Costa Rica, Panama and Guatemala — becoming more and more intrigued with the children as individuals.

"I liked the way that Latin America ChildCare kept us informed regularly of what was happening in the countries," says Mr. Murphree.

Mrs. Murphree would send cards and letters with little things like stickers, pictures, or a packet of seeds ... anything that fit in an envelope that she thought that they might like. And the children would always write back — they loved the mail and the attention. Relationships were built with each child individually, over time.

The impact that this couple is making in the lives of 16 youths through Latin America ChildCare is astounding. Emilce's school is in the most criminal part of Paraguay's capital city. Drug and alcohol abuse is rampant in the area and many of the children have suffered physical abuse. But Emilce wants to be just like her teacher when she grows up, reaching out to help others in need.

Then there is Ruth, a teenager who attended junior high, and now senior high in the LACC school system. Ruth wants go to college and study psychology, with her ultimate goal to become a missionary. The Murphrees have had the opportunity to witness the blossoming of a child to a young woman as Ruth has matured during their sponsorship.

Magdalena Maidana de Curvas, Ruth's Spanish grammar teacher, is a favorite with the Murphrees. The personal time and training this special teacher has invested in Ruth's life set a strong Christian example for Ruth to follow.

This one couple has secured the futures of 16 children so far through LACC, offering them education and training, wisdom and security, and a strong foundation in Christ. "Our prayer is that these children will grow into fine Christian men and women for the Lord," shares Mr. Murphree, "because of the partnership of Latin America ChildCare, the dedicated teachers and all the caring sponsors!"

Katia's Bright Future

Katia Beatriz was a child in need from one of the poorest barrios in El Salvador. The likely future that her dismal community offered her was drugs, violence, and probably prostitution.

Surely, she could never have gained an education, or found her way out of the endless, bitter cycle of poverty, except for the compassionate support that allowed her to become a student at an LACC-supported school.

Her teacher, Professor Jose Gilbert Velasquez, is from Katia's own area, so not only does he know what he is up against, he is thoroughly devoted to his students' success. Working in the barrios, he is using his Christian witness to bring hope and understanding to the children that he teaches.

Michael Mancari of Akron, Ohio, his wife Phyllis, and their three sons, Vincent, Jordan, and Justin, as a family, contribute $28 a month so that Katia can have the opportunity to go to a school sponsored by Latin America ChildCare.

The Mancari's boys understand that they are helping to provide an excellent education — and daily opportunities to meet the Lord Jesus and to grow in Him. Even if they never meet face-to-face, their $28 a month sponsorship made it possible for Katia to know Professor Velasquez, and that relationship is changing this little girl's life forever.

Professor Velasquez will never let go of Katia, demonstrating daily that being the daughter of a King means you have a bright future, no matter where you live.

God's Garden at the Dump

Juarez, Mexico, is just across the border from El Paso, Texas — close enough for the children of Juarez to see the bright lights and tall buildings of the American city. This vista is viewed while standing amid cardboard huts and reeking garbage piles that are home to thousands of Mexican children.

It is to this cesspool that God brought dignity, education, and His salvation message, through a man named Martìn Rubio.

Martìn is a schoolteacher; in fact, he comes from a whole family of schoolteachers. When he came to Christ a few years ago, his first concern was how he could use his teaching skills in service to Jesus.

He decided to build a school for the children who played around a nearby garbage dump — and recruited five of his own family members to teach there.

Martìn remembers the first time he looked on that dump, with its heaping piles of broken glass and plastic bags. Standing there, he felt that God was speaking to him, saying:

> *Each plastic bag is like a flower, waiting to bloom. Each broken piece of glass is like a diamond in the rough, waiting to be polished and shined. And that is what these children are, Martìn, flowers and diamonds.*

At the same time, God was moving another heart in Juarez. Pastor Padilla, who saw restless, impoverished children passing his church every day — on their way to play at the garbage dump — felt a burden to reach them with the academic basics of reading, writing ... and redemption!

He also employed Martìn's help in opening a school in his church, and enlisted his seven children as teachers. Today, that school is teaching academics and the love of Christ to 400 children every day.

So far, Martìn and his family have been instrumental in helping Assemblies of God churches launch two kindergartens, five primary, and two secondary schools in some of the poorest areas of this border city.

Today, Martìn is pastoring one of the Assemblies of God churches and directing one of the Latin America ChildCare schools ... a school located in the heart of one of Juarez' largest garbage dumps!

Thanks to the tireless efforts of the Rubio family, over 1,000 children are not only getting a real education — but also hearing every day how much God loves and cares for them.

These men followed the direction and guidance of the Holy Spirit within them, and affected sweeping changes that provided hope, practical skills, and an introduction to Christ for thousands of lost and directionless children.

Martìn Rubio and Pastor Padilla are much more than just shining examples of what God can do with one person — they are the Almighty's challenges to us!

Knowing this, how can we avoid asking ourselves, "What is God telling ME today?"

Prayer and Bravery

When the El Salvadorian government proposed to change their current ban on abortion, the legislature invited Eileen Romero, one of our LACC children, to address the entire assembly and give her opinion.

Eileen is a good student, and a devout Christian. She also suffers from some significant birth defects. As a young, educated Christian woman overcoming limitations on a daily basis, Eileen was eminently qualified to speak on this subject.

As you can imagine, speaking to an assembly of her nation's lawmakers was not something she had ever imagined herself doing. She was pretty frightened. She prayed, and knew others were praying. She also knew that she was the only one who could say what she came to say, so she bravely faced her nations' leaders and declared:

> *I recognize that I am physically imperfect, and my mother could have had an abortion rather than have a deformed child. But even though I am deformed, I am made in the image of God, so I have human dignity, and my life is worthwhile. God has given me a purpose in my life, and I am glad that my mother chose to give me life.*

Simultaneous to Eileen's speech, her classmates from Latin America ChildCare schools all around El Salvador joined in rallies to support the current laws against abortion.

The students also created "una cadena de oración" — a prayer chain. The children prayed in two-hour shifts all day at school, and then right after school they went on evangelistic missions in their neighborhoods.

As a direct result of the prayers and protests of Christian adults and children across the country ... and Eileen's bravery in speaking out about what was right ... the unborn of El Salvador remain protected.

> *Students created "una cadena de oración" — a prayer chain*

Even though they are children, our students understand that they helped to make a difference. Now they know that it isn't how old they are, but how holy and powerful their God is, that matters in the end. So there can be no limit to what can be accomplished in His will.

Imagine the powerful impact these children will have as they grow in the faith and become the adult leaders of their nations!

And the glory is to Almighty God who created a plan for loving and sustaining His children through the sponsorship programs, education and nurturing of Latin America ChildCare.

The Meeting of Two Cultures

Exciting news traveled through the tiny school: Zynthia's sponsors were coming from the United States, to meet her and visit with her family!

The seven-year-old danced delightedly, but as the day approached she was frightened too. What would they be like? Would they like her? They spoke a different language, so how could she talk to them?

Dick and Violet McKinley of Zephyrhills, Florida, finally arrived in Panama City, where missionaries Rod and Sherry Boyd greeted them and conducted them to Dolequita, Panama. The six-hour drive-time provided the McKinleys with a lot of information about the little LACC-sponsored school, where they were about to meet a child they already adored from her letters.

Two years previous, Zynthia has been among the first class of first graders. The plan had always been to slowly create a primary school by adding a new grade every year. But funds had not been found to establish a third-grade class for the 35-student school in Dolequita. It was beginning to look as though two years of schooling was all these children could be offered.

The implication for little Zynthia was apparent. If funding wasn't found to start a third-grade class, her years of schooling were nearly over. Much troubled by this information, the McKinleys turned their attention to meeting and getting to know their sponsored child. Of course, it was love at first sight!

The children of the school had gone all out, donning traditional costumes and performing in song and dance, in honor of the sponsor's visit. The school director, and Zynthia's teacher, Derila, visited with the Americans. By the end of the day, Zynthia's family had invited the couple to their home, where she introduced them to her parents, an older sister and a younger brother.

The embracing of American and Panamanian was a whirlwind for the McKinleys. Missionary Rod Boyd describes the experience: "It's hard to describe this meeting of two cultures. We were reminded once again of the humble lifestyle in Panama, a small, simple home on a dirt road filled with pot-holes. As we left, the Panamanian family expressed their thanks for the finances that allowed their daughter to attend school — and the family from Florida said it was their honor to do so."

The McKinleys departed deeply concerned for their little Zynthia and all her second grade classmates who were literally running out of school to attend. Back in Florida, Dick and Violet created a fundraiser to help the school at Dolequita continue growing and serving more children. They also decided to sponsor a second child at the school.

Joy and fulfillment shine from every angle when sponsors and students meet. And even though it is not something we plan, it is not unusual for sponsors like the McKinleys to become even more involved with the schools, after experiencing the quality of education, spiritual growth, and loving personal care firsthand.

We Are Blessed to Be Blessings

by Heather Reid

Oscar is a student at an LACC-sponsored school, but he is really only eight years younger than I. Upon meeting this amazing young man, my mind is challenged by the obvious similarities and contrasts of our lives.

When I was little, I used to go to preschool and my mom proudly displayed my scribblings with a magnet on the refrigerator door.

When Oscar was little, he came home one day to find his mother trying to poison herself.

And by the time Oscar was 16, his father had sold the family's home and left them.

Today, when I sent an email home to my brother, I was thinking of how he will graduate from college in another year. As opposed to

Oscar who works long hours in a restaurant to pay for the tiny apartment where he lives and supports his brother — who is a dedicated drug addict.

Overcoming obstacles is such a part of Oscar's life, he barely questions it anymore. It takes him three hours to get to his computer class by bus every weekend. All week long, he holds down a job and also attends his LACC-sponsored high school ... one that he fears he may be forced to leave before the end of the term if he can't make ends meet.

But he believes that God will provide.

And I believe it too. And I tell him so. But my heart feels raw.

How could my brother and I have been so lucky? What did I do to deserve my life? And an even more disturbing thought: what did Oscar do to deserve his?

Nothing. I realize these are choices that God made before any of us were conceived, and no one else needed to be consulted — and also that these are the questions that mankind has stumbled over for thousands of years. I'm grateful that being a believer allows me to know that there are answers, even if I will never know what they are.

Then I remember something that I was told when I was a new Christian:

"We are blessed to be blessings."

Who will be a blessing to Oscar?

Oscar needs a sponsor who will make sure he can finish high school and continue onto the university. He dreams of studying computers. And right now all I can do is pray for him and believe...

... that God's beautiful plan for the life of this young man will unfold, and Oscar's love for Jesus, and his cheerful resourcefulness will be rewarded somehow.

As I pray, I suddenly see the obvious ...

... Oscar is already living proof of what God's will can accomplish in a seemingly hopeless situation.

Uzziel's Success

Dorothy Cederblom, a missionary to Panama, who has worked closely with Latin America ChildCare for years, shared a powerful story about a young man named Uzziel:

> *He who goes out weeping, carrying seed to sow, will return with songs of joy, carrying sheaves with him. Psalm 126:6 is a Bible verse that has special significance to us as the school year ended for our Good Shepherd School at Las Mañanitas, Panama.*
>
> *Thirteen years ago we opened this school in a needy area just outside Panama City. The children who were a part of that first kindergarten class now were the first to graduate from our high school on December 18. Among them was a young man named Uzziel Sierra.*
>
> *Uzziel was a bright-eyed little boy who always gave me a hug whenever he saw me on campus, and things went along well for several years. However, when he was in sixth grade his behavior was so unacceptable that he was expelled from school.*
>
> *His frantic mother pleaded with us to give Uzziel another chance. His father had just been released from prison where he had spent time for drug dealing, all of which precipitated the trauma and change in Uzziel. Now all the family was attending church and trying to put their life together. After many tears and prayers, he was readmitted with the promise that he would make a real effort to study and behave.*

Over the years Uzziel demonstrated a remarkable spiritual change in his life and he did well in his studies, so much so that he plans to attend university to study journalism. All the effort and love spent on this child, now a young man, have reaped a harvest of good. We trust that Uzziel will have a wonderful ministry as a great Christian writer for the glory of God.

The work of Latin America ChildCare continues to give academic and spiritual guidance to thousands of students like Uzziel, who are finding faith in God and opportunity in their lives because of caring people who provide scholarships for them. We praise God for His life-changing power!

The Path to a Bright Future Starts in ... "Misery"

Costa Rica's largest newspaper, *La Nacion*, calls these barrios, "Towns of Misery."

The students of the Latin America ChildCare-sponsored schools in four such communities ignore such indictments. They are busy turning these slums into cities of hope!

One of these barrios is Los Cuadros, home to the largest Latin America ChildCare school in Costa Rica. Founded in 1985, the school serves 1,300 children and teens. Already former students have begun forging careers for themselves in medicine, law, business and government. And the same dedication exists in the current students.

Part of the explanation for the success of the school in Los Cuadros is the wide range of skills taught there. A good example of this is the industrial arts area of the high school which already employs some of the barrios' young men. The program has taught the school's boys the rudiments of construction — the students make or repair about 300 desks per year — using the finished products in their own classrooms.

During school breaks, the complex remains open and many young men of Los Cuadros build other things that they sell to earn a living. About 100 students a day work in this program.

Irine Sanchos is a new graduate of the high school at Los Cuadros, and at 18, she has just begun her freshman year at the University of Costa Rica, studying Economics and Agriculture.

Reflecting on her old school and her new one, she says, "It's a different world. At Los Cuadros, everyone always gave so much attention to every student. I have the basics for a good education, so moving on is not difficult, but I miss the teachers' concern for our education as well as our spiritual and home life."

Former students forge careers in medicine, law, business and government

Amazingly, Irine's family is Catholic, and her friends wondered why her parents allowed her to attend an evangelical Christian school, but Irine says, "I loved hearing about the Lord. I listened to all that was said and put it into practice."

Although Irine and the other students of Los Cuadros may have come from a "Town of Misery," God has raised them up and set them on the path to a bright future in Him.

Ramona Says Thank You

Ramona Diaz graduated from the Latin America ChildCare program years ago, but recently she wrote a thank-you letter, intended for her sponsor Dave Morgan.

She said, "Three years ago, I was in high school, but now I am in San Paul's Secretarial College at the university. In my church, I am a member and the director of the pantomime group that does drama outreach. Besides that, I am director of Sunday School."

Ramona was like millions of poor children across Latin America, a girl who might have had little to hope for and believe in if someone had not stepped in to enable her to go to school and develop in her walk with Jesus. Yet now, there is hope for her and her whole family.

"I live with my grandmother, and I love her so much," Ramona wrote to her former sponsor. "My grandmother and I are both very grateful to you, and my desire now that I am in the university is to thank you."

She signed her letter, "Sincerely and thankful."

This is the kind of life-changing difference that can be made for a sponsored child. The "lost generation" of Latin America can be found and saved, one life at a time, with the help and prayers of people who care!

Coralia, The Defender

When nine-year-old Maria arrived on our Latin America ChildCare campus, she had been so abused by her father that she could barely talk, or even walk.

Surely Maria had hoped going to school would supply some relief for her, even if it just meant being away from home more. And she hoped that school would be a safe place where she would not be hurt by anyone.

But what she could not have guessed when she became assigned to Coralia's class was that God had raised up a godly, gutsy defender-of-children to change her life.

Coralia was horrified and outraged at the child's condition — and went directly to Maria's home. There she confronted the father, letting him know that the abuse had to STOP.

Furthermore, the father was to understand that Coralia was going to be scrutinizing Maria's physical condition every day at school … and she would not shrink from notifying the police if she found even one sign of mistreatment on her student's body.

That incident served to relieve much of Maria's home pressures, and the good food and medical care at the LACC-sponsored school would begin to repair her other physical needs.

Maria now spends every day working by Coralia's side in class. She can never forget the compassion and concern that her teacher exhibited on that first day.

Through their friendship, Maria has learned that Jesus loves her and has provided for her a relationship with a loving Heavenly Father.

And when Coralia was asked why she was willing to be so bold and risk herself so much for a student in her class, the response is immediate, nearly indignant: "I do it because God has called me to do it! I have no other choice!"

Making Her Life Count

The Guarani Indians live in the most remote areas of Bolivia. This small ethnic minority has been relegated to the worst poverty and darkness in one of the poorest nations on the continent. But several years ago, through friends and sponsorships, a new school was built for the Guarani children.

Lidia is one of the sharpest and most motivated of all the graduates of the LACC-sponsored school in her village of Samaria, and she had completed 6th grade, the last grade available at her village's school. But she decided she wasn't through learning yet.

When she asked if she could continue her schooling at the nearest Latin America ChildCare facility — the junior high school at Freedom School near the Palmasola Prison — this just didn't seem possible.

Lidia was adamant that this needed to happen and ultimately this is what she and her mother worked out in order for this young lady to further her education: in the morning Lidia walks five miles to the bus stop, where she catches her ride to school. She arrives for the 2 P.M. session, has her meal with the other students, and then begins classes.

Classes finish at 6 P.M., then Lidia catches her bus back. Because the buses are crowded with workers headed home, it sometimes takes until 9 P.M. for her to get a seat on a bus. Her mom waits for her each evening, and together they make the five-mile hike home, in the dark.

Lidia's day ends about 10:30 or 11 P.M.

And she doesn't mind a bit. It means she can receive an education, and education is key to her future because Lidia has felt God's call on her life.

Veteran missionary John Wilkie reports: "Lidia has told the director of Freedom school that she will do anything she can to learn. She is hungry for knowledge — and she wants to be a better Christian, a good wife, and a mother."

In fact, Lidia believes that the Lord will some day bring her into a marriage with a man who has been called to ministry, and together they will serve Him.

The investment that countless friends and sponsors have made in Latin America ChildCare has allowed tens of thousands of children like Lidia to receive an education and an introduction to Jesus.

"Most of all, Lidia wants to make her life count," John says, "And she isn't even 15 years old yet!"

God's Benevolent Provision for Venezuelan Children

The First Assembly of God in Des Moines, Iowa, presented Latin America ChildCare with the largest single offering it has ever received: a remarkable gift of $190,000 to help the Fuente de Vida (Fountain of Life) School in El Pauji, Venezuela.

The church, pastored by John Palmer, got the idea to help Fuente de Vida School in 1998 when Bob Steward, his wife Karen, and 27 church youth traveled to Venezuela. While working with Mary Mahon, missionary, and Alexis Mora, pastor of Fuente de Vida Church, they saw the foundation of the school.

After the group returned to Des Moines, Bob approached his church's board with the idea for a special project to raise money to help complete the school, and the congregation responded generously!

The church raised a $158,000 one-time gift in cash, and has since raised $32,000 more. In addition, the church has sent a 60-member construction team and medical team to El Pauji. Although the construction team got understandably side-tracked helping the community dig out of the most devastating natural disaster of the last century — a flood of incredible proportions — they will probably schedule another time to complete the school building!

Fuente de Vida School is strategically located in El Pauji, a community on the edge of Caracas, Venezuela, the capitol city. It is a barrio plagued with alcoholism, drug abuse, gangs and violence. But within this dangerous community are people who love God and want their children to have a bright future.

LACC's partnership with Fuente de Vida School is an awesome opportunity to impact lives forever through the building of this school. Children don't just learn the basics of reading, writing and arithmetic — they also learn about our resurrected Redeemer, our Lord Jesus Christ.

And as these students trust Christ and He changes them, their lives will be positively marked for now and eternity. These children will, in turn, change their families, their community and ultimately their country.

The recent floods in Venezuela have affected the community surrounding the Fuente de Vida School. Many of the children lost their homes, some are orphaned and tragically some died in the disaster.

At the same time, there are many open doors to share Christ's love to the flood victims. Children from the nearby public school that was destroyed are receiving classes at Fuente de Vida. And church members, many of whom have lost their homes, are mobilizing themselves to minister to children and their friends in government shelters.

The school provides a desperately-needed resource in an area wracked by destruction and despair. "Parents are very pleased and say their children are receiving a better education than they did in the public schools," says Pastor Alexis Mora of Fuente de Vida Church. "Most (of these children) in El Pauji are not attending any school."

> *There are many open doors to share Christ's love*

The future plans for the school (whenever this can be arranged again) include adding two more floors to provide additional classroom space, a library and a basketball court on the roof. The school may also add a small dental clinic.

Although now meeting the educational needs of young children, Fuente de Vida School hopes to someday also provide training for young adults, including secondary education and technical instruction leading toward a university education.

The future looks bright at Fuente de Vida School — Pastor John Palmer and the First Assembly of God in Des Moines responded to the urging of the Holy Spirit, and the miracle of God's provision bringing a message of salvation and blessing to the many needy people of El Pauji, and the horizon of opportunity to the youth of Venezuela.

Latin America ChildCare ministers during "Panorama of Death"

It started as a series of small thunderstorms off the coast of Africa ... but by the time Hurricane Mitch hit the coasts of Central America a few weeks later, it ranked among the most devastating storms in modern history — wreaking almost unimaginable destruction and killing 14,000 people.

Hardest hit were Nicaragua and Honduras, where up to two feet of rain a day fell on some areas. As the dying hurricane stalled over the region it brought deadly floods and mudslides of unprecedented magnitude.

Honduran President Carlos Flores Facusse grimly told his people, "We have before us a panorama of death, desolation and ruin throughout the entire country."

Across Central America, authorities struggled to find words to express the extent of the tragedy — which came less than six weeks after Hurricane Georges devastated the Dominican Republic in the Caribbean, leaving hundreds dead and hundreds of thousands homeless.

"I've seen earthquakes, droughts, two wars, cyclones and tidal waves," said Cardinal Miguel Obando y Bravo, Roman Catholic Archbishop of Managua, Nicaragua, the nation's senior religious figure. "But this is undoubtedly the worst thing that I have ever seen."

Almost no family was left untouched by the twin hurricane disasters, and in some cases the personal loss was staggering. One Nicaraguan lost 47 relatives of all ages.

> *One Nicaraguan lost 47 relatives of all ages*

In the Dominican Republic, virtually every road, bridge, and airstrip was damaged or destroyed. Hundreds of thousands were made homeless, with the accompanying food and water shortages and thousands of dead bodies strewn across the countryside, increasing the danger of epidemics.

The second poorest nation in the hemisphere, Honduras, lost most of its banana and coffee crops, estimated at $500 million, and 70 percent of its grain harvest, throwing tens of thousands of workers into unemployment.

Both storms brought tragedy of heart-breaking proportions ... and presented opportunities for Latin America ChildCare missionaries and staff to reach out in a powerful way to these shattered communities.

Here are some updates of devastation ...

Nelson and Rennae de Freitas, Missionaries to Dominican Republic wrote us with this:

> We are in extreme need. We know that our Latin America ChildCare kids have been greatly affected.
>
> We feel so blessed that (our schools) survived the storm without major damage. In at least two of the schools, this is due to the fact that they recently had MAPS construction teams put a cement roof on the building. Praise God for His provision!
>
> Because these schools are well-built, they are now being utilized as refugee centers for the families of the children, the church and the community.
>
> Our school in San Juan de la Naguana is a refuge for 400 people. In this region, the river literally wiped the towns of Mesopotamia and Guachupita off the map.

From Honduras we heard from Missionary Bill Stickland:

> More than 50 major bridges are out. Over half a million are in shelters without food, water or medicine. We have over 1,500 in the Bible school and desperately need funds to feed, clothe and treat them.
>
> In all my years, I have never seen anything like this. It will take years to rebuild the infrastructure, churches and houses. Many of our pastors have lost absolutely everything. Many churches are gone. More of our believers have lost everything.

And from Randy Bardwell, the LACC Regional Coordinator:

> School is probably over for the year. Five of our schools are being used to house the homeless and may be used for this for

> the next two weeks or so. These people include Latin America ChildCare children and families and others from the churches and neighborhoods.

Bonnie Carlyon, Missionary to Nicaragua wrote:

> The overflowing rivers have swallowed up many communities. We have heard that some communities have disappeared completely. Our Latin America ChildCare doctor went up towards Leon ... (and) came upon a scene where they were burying a family of six people. They had been holding on to a tree and could not hold on any longer. The whole family was found dead clutching on to each other.
>
> People are walking around with just the clothes on their backs in a state of shock. It really is a horrible situation.

Throughout the regions stricken by Hurricane Georges and Mitch, our Latin America ChildCare missionaries, staff, and teachers opened our schools as refugee centers, temporary shelters and distribution centers for food and clothing.

In many cases, our solidly-built schools were among the few structures left standing — and the kind outpourings of funds and support enabled us to ship more than 400 tons of critically-needed supplies to these facilities.

These supplies of food, clothing, medicine and safe drinking water — some of them donated outright, many of them purchased with generous gifts from supporters and shipped as quickly as possible — were nothing short of a miracle for many of our students and their families in storm-ravaged areas of Central America and the Caribbean.

We distributed this emergency relief to devastated communities in the name and loving spirit of Jesus Christ ... ministering His mercy to thousands of stunned and hurting people.

Our Latin America ChildCare missionaries, staff and teachers worked almost non-stop to help with the crucial relief efforts — often in the face of unnerving and deeply stressful circumstances. They asked for prayer to continue to minister to those grieving for the thousands lost, and continued to make themselves and our facilities available to those in need.

It's important to remember that the greater community of Latin America has been hit so hard by natural disaster as to wipe out communities and infrastructures — twice in recent memory.

Thus it is doubly important to reach the children of these nations with the Good News of God's love for them, as they are almost universally in need of special care and nurturing. Latin America ChildCare wants to meet their physical, emotional and spiritual needs in the name of Jesus.

Our students are the ones that will lead their nations into the next decades, with Christ in their hearts, and change the face of Latin America for Him!

We are grateful to have been strategically placed so as to assist the families and neighborhoods in need in their times of trial. And we are equally grateful for the friendship and partnership in ministry that we share with our supporters, that makes it possible for LACC to bring food, clothing, medical supplies and comfort when disaster strikes.

United ... at long last

The story of Jaime Francisco Moreno Mejia is representative of the impact made on thousands of children through LACC. More than 30 years ago, he was a student at Liceo Rev. Juan Bueno Central in El Salvador. With the support of his sponsors, he attended kindergarten through eighth grade, encouraged all the way by letters, Christmas cards, and gifts on special occasions.

Jaime eventually went on to study electrical engineering, received an MBA in Business Counseling, and began his career. But he never forgot the love and care of his sponsors, whom he said helped lay a foundation for his present success at his company. He longed to meet them.

God gave him the opportunity when a business trip to Europe had a layover in Washington, D.C. Remembering that his sponsors had lived in that area, Jaime began an intensive search on the Internet for a Mr. and Mrs. Blaine. Just 15 days before Jaime's trip, he made a call — and Mrs. Blaine answered.

Jaime began explaining the long-distance call from El Salvador. But Mrs. Blaine, now in her 90s, was overjoyed. "Jaime!" she exclaimed. "It has been so long since we've heard from you!"

They cried together on the phone and Jaime found out that advancing age had blinded Mr. Blaine. But they were all rejoicing. "The Lord fulfilled one of my greatest desires which was to thank this family for blessing me," Jaime later remembered.

For 25 years, Jaime had kept a picture of the Blaine's house. That many years later, he finally arrived at the same house to a warm welcome. The hug he received, Jaime said, was one like he had never experienced before — full of unconditional love. They had lunch together, and Jaime thanked them for their sponsorship. His family had been blessed by the Blaine's help, he explained, and most of all, their sponsorship had given him the important foundation of his education.

During his brief visit, Mrs. Blaine showed Jaime a special treasure — a chest full of his letters, birthday cards, and thank you notes that Jaime had written them. Jaime was moved to tears.

"They treated me like a son"

"They treated me like a son," Jaime said.

Saying good-bye was difficult. God had brought these two families together through a need ... and now, 30-some years later, they finally had the chance to meet, face-to-face. As the Lord moves you to be a sponsor, you, too, may never know where or when you will meet your special child, maybe not until heaven — but you can know that your love and support is providing an excellent education, and a feeling of love, hope, and closeness to a child in need.

Conclusion

If you have felt a lump in your throat as you read through these pages ... if a little Yelitza, Lisbeth, Carlos or Juanito has pulled at your heart strings, then we ask you to remember: their stories are still being told. We gave you a short glimpse into a certain touching episode of their lives, but those same lives are still being lived.

Some of the children you've read about here are doubtless grown up by now, like Jaime, and many of them have gone off to college, then returned to the barrio to work double shifts in a Latin America ChildCare school as a teacher or director, to help other children escape lives of poverty and hunger.

Others are teenagers now, living lives of Christian faithfulness, young men and women who have felt God's call on their lives and in the near future will become the ministers and evangelists to keep the revival alive in Latin America as the Spirit works through them. And of course we believe that one day one of our students will rise to leadership of their nation.

Those stories are still waiting to be told ... and the wonderful part is, you may still be part of their stories! The story of Latin America ChildCare and the children we serve will never end, and we would love for you to tell your part of the story, too. How can you do it?

You can pray! Every great ministry begins with someone's prayers. The pastors whose churches work side-by-side with the schools pray without ceasing. The teachers who give such huge amounts of their time, love and compassion — they also pray. The school administrators, the staff of Latin America ChildCare, and the missionaries throughout Latin America, we all pray.

But the prayers of our sponsors, and the prayers of partners like you, make a wonderful difference. Sponsors who pray daily for their special children send God's love and the power of their faith directly into that young life. Partners who pray for the children, the teachers, and the churches and schools also send their love and compassion, too. In the spiritual warfare for the souls of Latin America's next generation, prayer is our greatest weapon.

Please pray.

There are still thousands of children in Latin America and the Caribbean that need to know Jesus and need the tools to break the chains of poverty — things that Latin America ChildCare provides.

The prayers of partners like you make a wonderful difference

As a sponsor, we invite you to become an advocate for the children. Your faithful sponsorship of a child means that you have taken God's love seriously. We invite you to talk to others about how they too can show God's love to a child — and make a difference in that child's life. Or you might want to participate in a sponsor's trip to see the schools personally — and meet your child. And you can become a volunteer to partner with LACC in changing lives, families and communities.

If you have thought about one day sponsoring a child, it's just $28 per month per child, but as you have seen in the pages of this book, that provides life transformation. A quality education in a Christian environment can serve as a springboard out of poverty. But an introduction to Jesus as Savior means a transformation that impacts that life for eternity. What better gift could you give? You can help write the story of the next young life to be transformed. This book is just the beginning! We appreciate your help and prayers more than you can know.

Notes

Notes

Notes

Make her smile last for an eternity

Francesca can smile today because someone like you cared.

She is one of thousands of youngsters in schools sponsored by Latin America ChildCare — and because of her sponsor's monthly $28 gift, Francesca receives things like nutritious meals, medical attention, a solid education to bring her out of poverty, and most importantly, the opportunity to meet Jesus Christ.

Please call or write TODAY for more information, or to say you'll become a sponsor. You'll make your own special child smile!

Call toll free: **1.800.289.7071**
Or check out our website at:
www.lacc4hope.org

Latin America ChildCare

Latin America ChildCare Sponsor Enrollment

❏ Please send me more information on sponsorship.
❏ I would like to sponsor a ❏ boy ❏ girl ❏ whoever needs me most.
I have enclosed: ❏ first month's gift of $28 ❏ annual gift of $336
❏ Please send me more information about giving a gift annuity.

NAME _____
ADDRESS _____
CITY _____ **STATE** _____ **ZIP** _____
PHONE ( ) _____ **E-MAIL** _____

Thank you for your love and generosity. All gifts are tax deductible as allowed by law. Please make checks payable to Latin America ChildCare, 1445 Boonville Ave., Springfield, MO • 65802-1894. E-mail Address: office@lacc4hope.org Website Address: www.lacc4hope.org

A MINISTRY OF ASSEMBLIES OF GOD WORLD MISSIONS